COWPER COUNTRY

Gordon Osborn

October 1977.

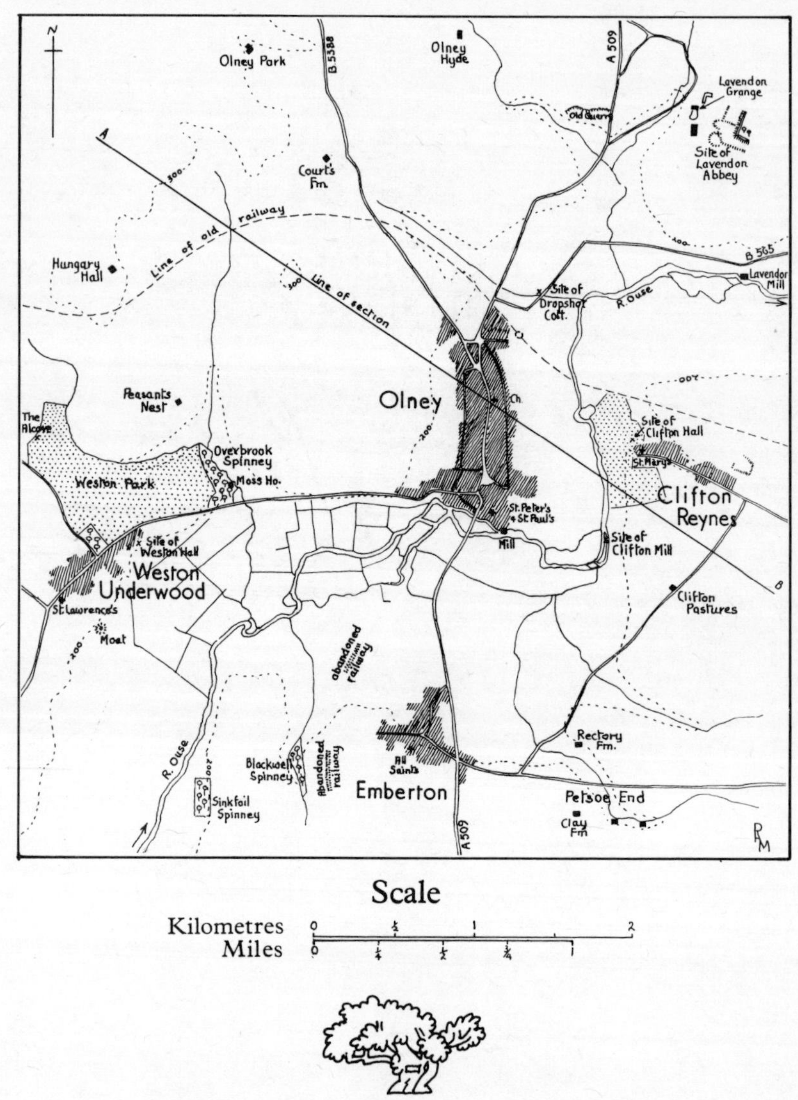

Scale

Kilometres					
0	½	1		2
Miles				
0	¼	½	¾	1

Map of the area around Olney

COWPER COUNTRY

an introduction
to the town of
Olney
and the
immediate
neighbourhood

by
GORDON OSBORN
F.L.S.

ACKNOWLEDGEMENTS

My thanks are due to the many people who have loaned books and photographs; and to others who wittingly or even unwittingly helped with information. Special thanks to Mr. George Knight for placing his knowledge of the area at my disposal. Thanks are due to Mrs. Van Horrik for typing and help in research, to Mr. R. A. Martin for reading the typescript and drawing the map and the section, and to Mrs. Ruth Bean for technical advice.

© 1976 by Arthur Gordon Hugh Osborn, F.L.S.

ISBN 0 9505530 0 X

Published by A. G. H. Osborn, "Pangea", West Street, Olney, Bucks. England.

Design by Paul Torr

Printed by Cheney & Sons Ltd., Banbury, England.

FOREWORD

Apart from my birthplace, where I lived for the first twenty-one years of my life, I have lived in Olney longer than anywhere. My work has taken me to the west, north and east of England. In two small market towns I have truly felt at home and in both I have felt I managed by some strange alchemy to have been absolved from the need to live the required twenty five years before one can claim citizenship. The first was perhaps because I found my wife there; the second, Olney, is because, in a way undreamed of, I found myself.

When I had been here a year or two it was decided to produce a pageant to celebrate the 200th anniversary of the Northampton Baptist Association to which, as a Church, we belonged. I was asked to take part and was told there was only one part for me, that of John Sutcliff, my illustrious predecessor, who figured so largely in the formation of the Baptist Missionary Society. I discovered then I knew very little about our early history or that of the town. Over the weeks of rehearsal I 'became' John Sutcliff. It was a strange experience, but I saw everything thereafter with new eyes – I had found myself.

Since then I have re-lived many past episodes of our church's and local history; I have been with Edward IV at the Bridge or Andrew Fuller and John Sutcliff at the Warrington crossroads; or have felt aggrieved with those non churchgoers who were bullied by local employers and heard the knock on our barn door of the arresting militia because a forbidden conventicle was meeting. I have walked with Joseph Kent and Cornelius Soul, with Georgina Masson and Judith Osborn (an ancestress of the author) some of whom were arrested for unlawful assembly and all involved in turbulent days in this small town. John Bunyan has been my companion and John Gibbs my inspiration – 'we meet' Hebrews says 'with the spirits of just men made perfect'.

When I bought a book on Isaac Watts (from a shop in Ludgate Hill) I said to the young man 'We wrote to him asking his help'. He was singularly unimpressed, but revised his opinion of me, with grave doubts about my sanity, when he realised I meant Isaac Watts. After all that is the only way to treat history.

All of this means Olney is a part of me and I feel, in a way I have never felt elsewhere, that I am inextricably involved with this small country town which has made such a contribution to the life of the world and my own.

Mr. Osborn seems unwittingly to have confirmed my feelings by asking me to write this introduction. It is truly an honour, which I find most humbling. I am grateful and wish this little book deserved success. May it confirm many in their love for this lovely, peaceful, healing place and give some new insight into its long life, which reaches out and touches us.

PETER GRAVETT
BAPTIST MINISTER.

CONTENTS

LIST OF ILLUSTRATIONS

INTRODUCTION

Almost without exception people visiting Olney say "What a charming place". Even those who have lived here all their lives must admit that, whatever its faults or failings, it has a charm not given to many towns of its size.

With the expansion of Olney, and the many newcomers, it is hoped this book will prove that, apart from being pleasant and pleasing to the eye, the Town and the surrounding district has much more to offer. The area described is quite small, about one-and-a-half miles radius from the Market Square – this includes Clifton Reynes, Emberton and Weston Underwood – easily reached in an afternoon's walk and providing a wealth of interest to anyone prepared to look for it.

It is not a complete history of the area, much else has been written, and in the years to come much more will be written. It is hoped it will fill a need for those who wish to know more of this area; also it has recorded events and facts which would be lost in the course of time.

During the past two thousand years many events have taken place here, probably a more varied history than almost any other comparable district. One must always look to the future, at the same time not forgetting the past, during which people and events have shaped the World in which we now live.

GORDON OSBORN 1976.

CHAPTER ONE
The structure and physical features

Looking at the area, the main feature is the wide river valley of the Great Ouse (Ouse is a pure Celtic river name) which swings round the town on the south and east sides and, in doing so, forms right angles so typical of this river.

To the north west is high ground, rising to about 300 ft. above sea level. This high ground continues toward Yardley Hastings in Northamptonshire. Across the river valley to the east there is high ground again, a continuation of the formation found on the north west side.

This part of the country is a stable area; an earthquake occurred on 22nd April, 1844, and another was felt as far as can be remembered in the early 'thirties.

It is possible that these geographical features and their geological basis have played an important part in the original siting of Olney, as well as the surrounding villages. Walking round the district it is noticeable how they are sited in the valleys; even Clifton Reynes although on top of the hill is situated in a hollow. The exception is Emberton, situated on the two hundred foot contour and on the north face of the hill dipping down towards the river. A look at the village from across the valley at the top of Weston Hill shows how well it snuggles into the hillside. Many villages throughout the Country owe their existence to some geographical feature such as a sheltered valley, or a good supply of spring water, or to a patch of sand or gravel in a clay area.

The high ground to the north west is bounded on the south side by the road to Weston Underwood and on the east side by the road to Warrington. This area includes the Peasants' Nest farm and the Court's farm. Also running through the area is the now disused railway line that linked Bedford and Northampton. This line was opened on June 10th, 1872. South of the Court's farm, and across the old railway lies the highest point in the area described, where there is a small patch of ground that is just over three hundred feet above sea level.

All the rocks are in what is known as the Jurassic System laid down under the sea about one hundred and seventy million years ago. Since then they have risen above sea level and have been subjected to the effects of the weather for millions of years. At one period the chalk lay on top, but that has since been weathered away re-exposing the older rocks underneath. Although within the Jurassic system of rocks, the oldest strata such as the Lower Lias and the Middle Lias are not represented, nor are the youngest rocks such as the Oxford Clay, the Corallian, and the Portland Series. The oldest rock here is the Upper Lias clay; above that there is the Oolitic Limestone, now re-named the Blisworth Limestone. This includes what is known as the Forest Marble, so called after the forest of Wychwood in Oxfordshire where it is well developed. On top of that is the Cornbrash which is on the high ground; in fact the Cornbrash escarpment runs along the top of Clifton Hill. This formation can be followed across the Country from Dorset to Yorkshire. It gets its name from the fact that it is a good corn growing formation.

Much of the high ground is covered with what is known as the Boulder Clay, also sometimes called till or drift. This material has been left by the great ice sheets that covered this Country during the Ice Ages. During the past one million years Northern Europe has been subjected to at least four glacial periods. At these times the country was under an ice cap similar to Greenland and Antarctica today. The most severe glaciation was the third one called the Riss glaciation, or to give it its English name, the Gipping Glaciation. This Boulder Clay is very thick in some areas such as Salcey Forest where it is about ninety feet thick; generally here it varies from none at all, to twenty or thirty feet thick. The new reservoir at Weston Lodge in Weston Underwood is built entirely in the boulder clay. This deposit has consideraby altered the topography from what it was before the Ice Ages.

Not only have the clay deposits altered the scenery, the melting waters from the ice sheet played their part and this water carved out the wide river valleys, which now have a small river flowing in the bottom. These small rivers in the large valleys are called "Misfits", and this is typical of most river systems in Great Britain as well as on the Continent.

Much of the Boulder Clay is that known as the Chalky Boulder Clay, due to the fact that it contains a lot of chalk picked up as the ice sheet moved across the North Sea and the chalk areas of Norfolk and Lincolnshire, eventually stopping at the Chiltern Hills, although in one place it passed over them and a lobe of the ice sheet extended as far as Finchley in North London.

As well as chalk in the clay many other types of rock are found; like the chalk these rocks were picked up by the ice as it travelled across the surface. A study of these pieces of rock tells an interesting story. The gravel pits at Emberton yielded many rocks from Norway and Sweden, many of them igneous or fire-formed rocks, as well as what are known as metamorphic rocks, that is rocks which have been changed or altered by heat or pressure or by chemical methods, or even a combination of these. These strange rocks or "erratics" as they are called, consist of such types as granites, mica schists, quartz porphyries, gneiss and basalt, as well as rocks from the north of England such as carboniferous limestone and immense quantities of Millstone Grit, from the Pennines. One granite from Emberton has been traced back to a spot just outside the city of Oslo in Norway, and another from Sweden. Besides the rocks mentioned there are vast quantities of flint and rounded quartzite pebbles. These pebbles, called Bunter pebbles, are from the Nottinghamshire area, and formerly used to make the pavements and the cobbled yards before they were replaced by blue bricks or concrete. They are called Bunter pebbles because that is the name of the geological formation from which they were obtained, and they are about thirty million years older than our rocks. A journey to Hanslope reveals a large erratic on the roadside at Tathall End by the side of the brook. This is a large boulder of olivine basalt. The basalt is a heavy black rock, the olivine in it occurs as small

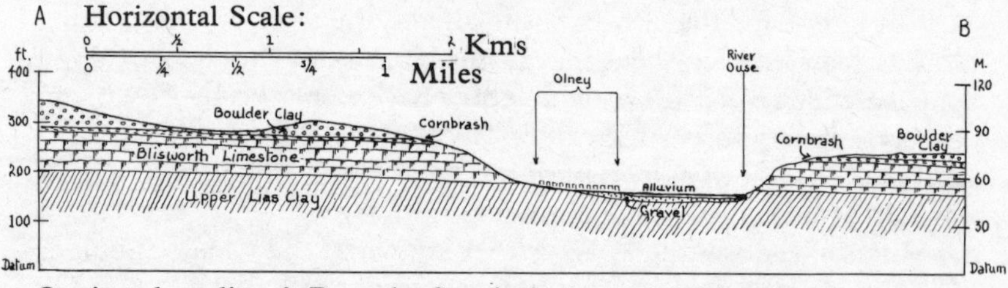

Section along line A-B on the frontispiece map of the area.

green crystals. This rock could have come from Derbyshire. Besides many specimens of this rock found at Emberton and other gravel pits in the area, there is one piece incorporated in the limestone wall that partly surrounds Clifton Court. It is mined in the north of England for roadstone, and it is the same material of which the Giant's Causeway is made.

The melt water from the ice sheet brought with it a huge load of stones, sand and silt; it is part of this material that has made the gravel deposits so sought after by the construction industry today. A look at the map shows that the main deposits are on the inside of the wide bends of the river valley. This is because the water flows faster on the outside of the bend and slower on the inside. This means that the slow running water, not having the energy to carry its load of gravel, then drops it where it accumulates as a gravel bank. At the same time, at the outside of the river bend, the water flows faster, and in so doing not only keeps the channel of the river clear but actually works away at cutting back the river bank. There are three examples of this to be seen, one on the Weston road where the valley swings from Tyringham. The slow flowing water was on the side of Emberton and the gravel it deposited has been extracted and holes left have filled with water to make the lakes in Emberton Park. At the same time, the fast flowing water on the outside of the bend has cut away the hill underneath the beech tree, making a steep hill from which a view is obtained of a wide part of the river valley to the opposite gravel bank with a very gentle slope up from the river. The same process has taken place to the east of Olney; the river has swung round,

4

deposited a large gravel bank on which much of the town is built, at the same time, undercutting Clifton Hill. The same process has occurred again at Lavendon Mill.

Another feature of this wide swift flowing river, which occurred about twelve thousand years ago, is that it deposited some gravel on the river banks. At first, with the initial flood of melt-water there must have been a time when the valley was very full of water. This left a river bank that can be seen today by careful observation; in fact, along the Lavendon Road part of the river, evidence of three of these river banks or river terraces as they are called, can be seen, one above the other. The terrace farthest from the river is the highest and the oldest one. These terraces and the gravel banks were used by the early inhabitants as somewhere to live on, and can be traced for miles along the valley of the Great Ouse, and many other rivers. The City of London started on the river terraces of the Thames.

The higher parts of the district consist of a limestone rock now called the Blisworth Limestone on top of which is found the boulder clay, although in some parts such as the Warrington road a thick band of clay is found near the top of the formation and immediately underneath the Cornbrash. This clay is called the Blisworth Clay, so named by Samuel Sharp in 1870, and in this part of the country it does replace what is known as the Forest Marble. This clay is a multi-coloured formation; generally a dark blue-grey colour it does have areas of brown and a purple colour. It is almost un-fossiliferous; there is often a band of fossil oysters at the bottom, otherwise it can be completely barren. Below this clay where it occurs the limestone is quite thick, in places over fifty feet. The limestone consists of many layers; some are layers of a hard limestone, other layers consist of sand and clay mixture. Other layers consist of a mixture of clay and limestone; this mixture is called marl.

Underneath the limestone is another clay formation, known as the Upper Lias clay. This clay does outcrop on the valley sides, and being impervious to water provides a spring line where the water soaking through the limestone emerges on the hillside at the top of the clay exposure. This spring line can be traced all along the north side of the valley. Starting along the Wellingborough Road there is a spring near where the old railway arch was, then comes the "Whirly-Pits". These do not dry up, as they are fed by the springs draining the water from the limestone to the north west. There is the spring at the horse trough in Yardley Road; the spring line then continues along West Street and crosses Spring Lane, or as it used to be called Spout Lane, a spring here being the source of the water for the stream that ran down the lane to the High Street, which went northwards and met a similar stream travelling in the opposite direction fed by a spring in the Yardley Road, probably the one that feeds the horse trough today. These two streams joined and turned towards the river where the United Reformed Church stands today. During the Middle Ages, it is said, the streams were used as open sewers, the rubbish thrown into them making it rather obnoxious during hot weather. There were willow trees on the banks, the banks being supported by a framework of wattle to stop them collapsing into the stream where the ducks nested.

Beyond Spring Lane the line of springs runs along the hill below the beech tree, up the sides of the valley cut by the Overbrook, then along the hill below Weston Underwood and on to Ravenstone Mill. The springs do not break out to the same extent on the other side of the valley; this is because the whole rock formation dips away towards the south east. This dip in the rocks is due to what is known as the Alpine Orogeny or mountain building movement. The Alps were formed by a gigantic push from the south. This folded the rocks up to form the Alpine range of mountains, at the same time pushing and folding the rocks of Europe and South East England.

The surrounding villages, too, have their geological interest. Weston Underwood is built on the limestone; the boulder clay here is very thin or non-existent. To the north of the village is an old stone quarry which, during recent years, has been opened again to provide material for the new city of Milton Keynes. This quarry has provided some useful information about the limestone in the area. The limestone exposed here is what is known as the "White Limestone"; this was determined by Mr. R. V. Melville of the British Museum. This quarry proved a thickness of rock to about sixteen metres, the Upper Lias clay being exposed lower down the valley sides.

From the quarry can be seen a valley that has been cut by the stream that runs down from the other side of the railway line. This stream goes down the valley to join the Overbrook at the north end of Overbrook spinney. It then continues towards the river, going under the road and producing what is known as an alluvial fan in the river valley. In doing this, the material brought down by the stream has built up so much that the stream itself is above the ground level as it runs across the meadows.

Emberton lies on a river terrace. Along West Pits, gravel used to be dug. Whether it is a glacial gravel or a river gravel is not known for sure, the possibility is that it is the latter. Petsoe End is a hamlet, which, nestling in a hollow, has a spring, and close by runs a stream. This stream is an obsequent stream as it runs down the face of the escarpment in the opposite direction to the main river.

Taking the road to Clifton Reynes the ground rises and the village is in a shallow valley bounded by the two hundred foot contour. Clifton is built on the limestone; there is almost no boulder clay. In the old quarry near the railway line there used to be a good exposure of the Forest Marble. This formation in this area does suddenly change its nature. At Bradwell it changes from hard rock to clay, the Blisworth Clay, while in Clifton the limestone is present and at Warrington the Blisworth Clay occurs again. This was proved in the new road cutting.

All these materials deposited here, cut and carved up by the action of ice and water over a long period, give a countryside that is pleasant to look at as well as to live in.

The main economic products of the area are limestone, gravel and clay. The limestone is a good building material; most of the old houses and farm buildings are built from it. The church is said to be built from stone excavated from what is known as the

"Dells", a field found up Long Lane. There is a depression which does look like an old quarry. The villages around had their own quarries; Emberton had one on Rectory Farm, Clifton and Weston Underwood had the quarries already mentioned. There was another large quarry along the Warrington Road. It is thought this provided much of the building stone for Olney. In the deeper parts of this quarry there was a good freestone, that is a stone that can be cut or sawn in any direction, not just in one plane. Many houses are faced with a dressed stone possibly obtained from this source. The limestone was also burnt to make lime; this was done at Warrington quarry where production ceased in 1910. Lime was also produced at the Clifton Quarry up to the 1930's. This quarry once belonged to the Wellingborough Furnace Company. It was then owned by a man called Gould and the lime produced was sold for about sixty new pence per ton. Last of all, it was owned by a Mr. Mattinson, a fine old north countryman, who farmed in Clifton. It ceased production before the second World War, when George Cooke was the last person to be employed there.

The gravel deposits are extensive and very much in demand. The meadows near the river are nearly all on a gravel deposit, the extraction of which would make an immense difference to the area. There is a large deposit between the Emberton by-pass and along the valley to Lavendon Mill, as well as up the valley towards Tyringham.

The other economic product is not now obtained locally, that is, the clay that was used to make bricks. The brick-yard at the Hyde Farm stopped making in 1910. There was a brickyard up the Weston Road near what is known as the Tan Cutting; the depression from where the clay was taken can still be seen, and the old cottages that once stood in the cutting were called the Brickyard cottages. In both these works the bricks were laboriously made one at a time by hand. An example of the bricks made at the Hyde can be seen in the south wall of 44 West Street.

Besides providing the scenery and the economic products the local rocks have produced good specimens of fossils, many of which can be seen in such places as the Sedgewick Museum in Cambridge, as well as in the local museum. The gravels have provided remains of mammoth and woolly rhinoceros, as well as ichthyosaur vertebrae. An interesting find at Emberton was of fossil wood which had been completely changed to silica, the material of which flints are made. Microscopical examination of this fossil wood shows the cell structure perfectly preserved. It must have been a local deposit, but exactly where has not yet been found out. Red deer antlers have been found; a nice antler was found in the Clifton meadows in 1971

Warrington has yielded many good specimens of fossils, most of which are in the Sedgewick museum at Cambridge. The recent road alteration provided a good series of Cornbrash fossils, from both the upper and lower Cornbrash. Another find here was a coral reef just beyond the lane to Lavendon Grange. The quarry at Weston provided many good specimens; here the fossil oyster *Liostrea hebridica* is found in abundance and in a good state of preservation. The thicker layers of rock contain many worm burrows which were made before the limestone hardened off. These are called Trace Fossils, *Diplocraterion*. The deeper layers revealed a layer of rock crowded with the brachiopod shell *Digonella digonides*. Specimens of this unique rock are in many museums and universities over the country.

Clifton Reynes has provided evidence of the Dinosaurs. The first was dug up in the quarry many years ago before the first World War; the next find was when the sewage system was put in. A trench in the limestone opposite the Robin Hood Inn yielded about a dozen pieces of bone, now, of course, turned to stone. It is thought the remains were those of a *Cetiosaurus* and these remains are in the Cowper Museum. It is understood that some bones were taken to Yardley Hastings many years ago but now they cannot be traced. The Upper Lias clay does yield fossils typical of that formation, but these can only be found when the clay is exposed. Nice specimens of *Dactylioceras Commune* were found in Emberton Park. An interesting deposit round here is coal; there is a six inch coal seam under the school on Moore's Hill and coal also occurs at the top of Weston Hill, at Warrington and at the

Pastures Farm where the remains of the coal shaft can be seen. In 1825 the Olney Coal Company was formed to mine this coal. On November 28th, 1825, it was resolved that if, after sufficient trials, it was not worth trying to work the coal the company should be wound up, and this was done. It was a Mr. Palmer who thought it would be possible to produce the coal and who was in charge of the trials. It is interesting to know that it was thought the coal would be worth from £1.10p. to £1.25p. per ton.

The other side of the valley the rock formation persists. The high ground from Newton Blossomville through Clifton Reynes and on towards Sherington is capped by the Cornbrash formation. Typical Cornbrash fossils can be picked up in ploughed fields here. An interesting find some years ago at Rectory Farm, Emberton, was an ammonite called *Choffatia (Loboplanulites) aff. Cerealis sp. Nova*. This ammonite figures in the Palaeontographical Journal for 1958.

During the past one hundred and seventy million years the rocks underneath us here have been formed and moulded by the processes of nature, to make this attractive corner of England which most of us take for granted – not giving a thought or asking the reason why it is so.

We need education in the obvious more than investigation of the obscure.

OLIVER WENDELL HOLMES.

CHAPTER TWO
Early History

Of the very early history of the district there is no written record. The first mention of the town is said to be in a charter dated 979 A.D. The treaty of Wedmore between King Alfred and Guthrum the Dane drew the boundary along the river, and Olney being on the north side came under Danish rule. At one time Olney belonged to a descendant of the Kings of Mercia, called Borret, or Borgret, who also owned properties in Bedfordshire and Northamptonshire.

Archaeological finds have proved that the occupation of the area went back much further in time.

There is, so far, no sign of any occupation of this area during the Old or the New Stone Age. Neolithic people did not settle so much in this area due to the clay deposits – they liked a lighter sand soil. Evidence of these people along the river valley is provided by finds at Biddenham, Kempston and Cardington, while recent excavations at Harrold show a site in the gravel between Harrold and Odell. A search of the material extracted from the gravel pits at Emberton revealed no evidence. Future excavations may prove that there were occupants of the valley here at that time.

Where the town got its name from is not known for sure. According to Oliver Ratcliff it is thought to be of Anglo-Saxon origin. The passage in the Charter says· "These are the boundaries of the ten hydes of land at Ollanege". Ege or Eg is pronounced "e" or "ey" from the Anglo-Saxon "ig" also pronounced "e"; this is said to mean an island or land nearly surrounded by water. The "n" in Olney is the Anglo-Saxon genitive of Ola. This suggests the origin of the name to be Ola's Island; Ola possibly being the name of some Saxon who owned the land.
Other suggestions are that the name is derived from Aln-ey, an

Romano-British pots found by the author at Emberton Park. *Photographs by Sidney Field.*

island of alder trees, or again the 1835 post-mark was Oulney thought to mean Ousen Eye, a wet place near the River Ouse. In Domesday Book the spelling is Olnei, and in the Civil War Tracts it is spelt Oulny. Another suggestion is that the Saxon EI means water, with no explanation of the origin of the first syllable. In the Grafton Chronicles it is spelt Wolney, and later in this book there is mention of it being spelt Olneye.

In Roman times Olney was a settlement as proved by the large amount of Romano-British pottery found. Ash Furlong, a field along the Lavendon road, has provided many Roman and early English coins from A.D. 90 to 325 A.D. As well as these coins Nuremberg counters have been found as well as seventeenth-century trade tokens. These can be seen in the Cowper Museum Also found in Ash Furlong was a statuette of the god Mercury, made of bronze. This was found by the late Mr. Gershom Longland and it is now in the British Museum. Coins have been found in the Near Town allotments. The late Mr. Jack Tunn found six

Roman coins on his piece of allotment there. Trenches for gas and water mains have revealed many finds. A pipe line excavation to Cold Brayfield revealed much Romano-British pottery including some Samian ware. Again roadworks at the sharp bend along the Lavendon road proved the existence of a medieval site extending under the road. In the field near the bend a piece of cut limestone with the letters T.B. was found. The digging of graves in the cemetery has yielded Saxon pottery, as did an excavation for a telephone cable in High Street South. An important find was of a medieval kiln site at the Hyde Farm, which has been excavated under Ministry of Works supervision.

Other villages also have evidence of early occupation, the most important find being at what is now Emberton Park. Much of this area is the site of a Romano-British encampment, but none of this showed on aerial photographs, due possibly to the thick covering of alluvium over the gravel in which the finds were made.

The first evidence there was of an archaeological site came from a workman who came to the author to say that an old fireplace

Carving of the god Mercury at the bottom of the well in Emberton Park. *Found and photographed by the author.*

had been found in the gravel. An examination of some of the stones proved they were covered with carbon, but there was no building for the fireplace to be in. Pursuing the matter it was proved the stones were used in the construction of a well and the carbon came from the decomposition of the algae which covered the stones in the well.

A few days later, word was received that a well had been found. As it was at the week-end the owners allowed until 8.30 on Monday morning for any digging to take place. Working through the week-end this pit yielded a quantity of pottery and right at the bottom of the well was found a limestone carving of the god Mercury. This well was between three and four metres deep and 0.83 metres in diameter, it extended only to the top of the gravel, and not into the alluvium. Soon afterwards another well was discovered, this

Looking down into the well excavated in Emberton Park, above the level of the carving of Mercury. *Photographed by the author.*

being only about 1.75 metres deep and about one metre across. This yielded a large quantity of cattle bones and some fine pots, as well as the remains of a leather sandal. More wells were discovered and yielded more pottery, including some decorated ware now in the County museum. These last wells were constructed on the same principle as was the first one to be found; they were about the same depth and exactly the same diameter.

In addition to the wells, the whole area was crossed with V-shaped ditches, some quite large and extending to the present boundaries of the Park. There was evidence of buildings and post holes were found, some in the typical ring formation, proving that at some time people had been living on the site. It is possible the site extends under the by-pass to the fields on the east side of the road.

Romano-British pots found by the author at Emberton Park. *Photographs by Sidney Field.*

Also found there, was a row of graves of soldiers who had perished in the civil war battle of Olney bridge.

Weston Underwood has an Iron Age site near to the village, and there are earthworks that might be of the same period. In 1858 in a field called White's Close a hoard of Roman coins was dug up and claimed as a treasure trove by Sir Robert Throckmorton. At the same place, there were pieces of Roman pottery and a quantity of bones as well. In recent years evidence of Romano-British occupation has been found in the area of Woodlands Farm and at Weston Lodge, as well as pieces of armour and weapons. Some of the ploughed fields show a scatter of stones, possibly the remains of buildings long since vanished.

Clifton Reynes has a Romano British site where the old quarry was, just over the old railway line. The working of the limestone destroyed the V-shaped ditches which crossed the top of the hill overlooking the river. Much pottery was found here, some of it being Salopian ware – a spindle whorl was also found. It is said

that a large quantity of pottery was buried in a pit, but efforts to find it have not proved successful. Within the village itself there are remains of an earthwork now almost obliterated. At Top Farm there is an almost square earthwork; the entrances to it are clearly defined, but like many others there is no history attached to it.

The river has also yielded many remains, including stone objects. Roughly shaped in the form of a hammer head with a hole through the shaft, some show signs of wear where a rope has been tied round them. As these objects are only found in the river, it has been suggested they are to do with fishing, probably weights for nets. They are found along many miles of river; quite a number of them were found at Old Stratford.

Also found in the river was a piece of Purbeck Marble which was carved, probably ornamenting the inside of some building The dry weather of 1975 provided conditions that showed the evidence of two hut circles on the Clifton side of the river opposite Lavendon Mill. The circles were shown to perfection in the ripe corn; where the post holes were the corn was about six inches taller than the rest of the crop.

Many gardens and ploughed fields, as well as almost any excavation in the area, yields something of interest, either from a geological or archaeological point of view.

CHAPTER THREE
Medieval History

The ecclesiastical and manoral histories have been well documented elsewhere, so there is no need to repeat them here.

The oldest part of the town is said to be the north end; this was originally called Townsend, and the hill up Yardley Road was called White Cross Hill, one of the springs near there being called Christian's Well. This was possibly the spring in the gardens at the side of Old's Lane. It was here that the church originally stood, this being built about 1018 A.D. The date is known because about 1800 repairs were carried out at the present church and during these alterations a beam was found with the inscription: "This beam was laid by Ben Marriot and Michael Hinde, churchwardens, July 17th, 1718, and 700 years from its first building (1018)". What was said to be the church yard elm stood opposite the house that used to be the Queen Hotel where Old's Lane meets the Wellingborough Road. The church yard was about where the houses stand in Feoffee Row, several skeletons having been unearthed there.

This could be where the early inhabitants made their first settlement, with the church nearby and a good supply of water from the springs; also standing a little higher than the valley and consequently not so damp.

Other evidence is that of Olney Mill which is mentioned in Domesday Book. At one time there was a mill at the bottom of Clifton Hill a few metres north of the footbridge across the river, and this has been called Clifton Mill but was demolished at the end of the 19th century. All that can be seen is where the mill stood and what used to be the mill race. A depression near the bridge is called the Witches' Grave. The old stone causeway across the meadow to where the mill stood has often been attri-

Olney church from a photograph taken by Mr. R. G. Scriven in 1876.

buted to the Romans, but it is more likely to be medieval, used no
doubt for horses and carts to cross the meadows which in winter
would be flooded or at least muddy and soft. There is a similar
causeway in Hanslope leading to where an ancient manor once
stood. The construction of this causeway is identical to that across
the meadows, and it could have been made by the same workman.

The bridges over the river along the Emberton Road have just
been widened, the big bridge recently being reconstructed in its
original style. The bridge was built in about 1832 and replaced

The churchyard elm drawn from an old photograph.

the bridge Cowper knew which was built in 1619. Cowper described this bridge in the "Task":

"O'er Yonder bridge,
That with its wearisome but needful length,
Bestrides the wintry flood."

It had twenty-four arches of various sizes and at irregular intervals. Each arch had a different name. The first arch was called the Constable Arch. There were wooden railings along the sides of the bridge, also stone steps to get down to the meadows.

During the recent reconstruction little was found of historical interest. This may be due to the fact that only a small area was excavated and this by mechanical means.

Many years ago, before the last World War, Turvey bridge was reconstructed and widened. During these alterations a Viking spearhead was found in good condition with an engraved pattern on the blade. Some time later a Norwegian loom weight was found at Lavendon Mills, where the ford used to be on the lane from Clifton Reynes to Lavendon Grange and beyond. These finds give some idea how far the Vikings penetrated inland by making their way up the rivers from the coast. This raises the question of what influence did they have on our early ancestors who were living in this area.

In the fifteenth century Olney was protected by a wall in which there was a strong gate, but there is no evidence where the walls stood or where the gate was. The walled part of the town was probably the south end since this end of the town assumed more importance when the Church was built. Near the Castle Inn is said to be the site of Olney castle, but again no evidence is left as to where it actually stood.

Emberton village has a lot that is not fully explained. One question being did the village at one time exist in the field on the west side of the church.

According to the Reverend Hulton, who was Rector of Emberton from 1922 to 1932, the village got its name from an Angle called EANBERHT or EANBEORHT. The name of Emberton

Olney bridge from an old engraving.

meaning Eangerht's farm. It was thought he came up the river in search of a better place to make a home. During that period many people from North Germany settled in Buckinghamshire, and it is thought that it is from these people that the name of the county originates. The article by the Reverend Hulton was written before the discoveries at the site of Emberton Park, which proved the area had been occupied at a much earlier date.

The now vanished villages of Ekeney or Okeney cum Petsoe have left no trace. Whether there were one or two villages is still not known for certain. There were, however, two churches – the church of St. Martin at Ekeney and the church of St. James at Petsoe. The site of St. Martin's is shown on the Ordnance map. It is an interesting fact that neither of these places were mentioned in Domesday Book, but a list of rectors can be found in the Lincoln College registers at Oxford. The list of the rectors of Ekeney started a few years before the Petsoe list. Ekeney list starts with Hugh de Newport in 1246 and the Petsoe list starts with Hugh who died in 1247 and was succeeded in that year by Robert de Elkington; the churches were united in 1459 and lasted until 1726. The earliest mention of the two villages is that of Petsoe in 1198. The village of Ekeney gives its name to the family who owned it, Sir Robert de Akeney, who besides his other offices was Lord of Lathbury and Little Filbury. The village of Lathbury exists today but there is no trace of Little Filbury, nor is it known where it was situated. Tradition has it that the village of Ekeney had seventeen tenements and was less than five hundred acres in extent. When the Church at Ekeney was demolished, the chancel was taken down and re-erected on the south side of Stoke Goldington Church and used as a chapel. An examination of the church at Stoke Goldington shows this very well. The windows are of a different pattern and it is obvious where it has been joined on to the church. It is not used as a chapel now, as it is the vestry.

In Saxon times there were two manors, one held by two thanes or thegns called Godric or Goding and Uluric or Ulric. The other manor being held by another thane called Alric. There seem to be two different accounts about these manors. The Reverend Hulton mentions Alric as having one manor and Uluric the other. Ekeney, also spelt Akeney or Okeney, is said to mean the Island of Oaks. For Petsoe there seem to be two ideas of the origin of the name. One is Pets Hoo or "Peter's Place", and the other explanation is that the name originated from Peot's spur of land. In 1379 it was spelt Pettesho in one account. In 1509 the two parishes combined to form Ekeney-cum-Petsoe.

In Ekeney churchyard it is said a priest lies buried with a gold chain round his neck. Also a barn at Petsoe Manor is said to have been constructed of stone from the church as well as having the church's weather-vane on the roof.

The present church at Emberton is similar in many ways to Olney church, the design and workmanship being very similar. The tower of Emberton Church was built by John Nordon, a brass to him in the church being dated 1410 A.D. In the chancel it is said that Sir Everard Digby of Gayhurst lies buried. It will be remembered he was beheaded for his part in the Gunpowder Plot.

It was at the end of July 1469 that Robin of Redesdale with 20,000 men stopped at Emberton, when he was marching to attack King Edward IV who had taken refuge within the walls of Olney. The King was captured and the battle called off. Remains from Robin's army have been dug up from time to time.

The tower in the centre of the village was erected by the Reverend Thomas Fry in memory of his wife. The clock in the tower and the bell (made by John Rudhall of Gloucester in 1806) were given by Miss Hughes.

The Reverend Fry drove his cart drawn by two donkeys in tandem; he died in Bath in 1860.

Emberton Manor is modern, being built in 1879. The old manor stood much nearer the road, but it was demolished and rebuilt in the present position. One of the windows from the old manor was taken out and used in the present building.

Between 1700 and 1750 there was a grocer, poulterer, lacemaker, mason, miller, dairyman, molecatcher, victualler, and a malster in the village. In Domesday Book it is recorded that there was 'Pannage" or foraging for sixty hogs in Emberton Woods.

The road between Olney and Emberton has seen a lot of history – not only military battles being fought there but legal ones as well. One was trying to decide who should pay to keep the bridge in repair. It was frequently damaged by floods and the verdict was that Olney should pay.

At the bridge called the "White Rails" along the Emberton Road the pool of water is called "Moll Houghton's Hole". There seems to be no explanation how this name originated, nor who Moll Houghton was.

At the entrance to the Park there used to be a field called "Frogs Hole" which contained a pond or part of a moat similar to one on Manor Farm. It is thought they might have been part of the defences of the village at one time.

To travel along the road a toll used to be levied, the collector who collected what was known as the Duchy Toll (Duchy of Lancaster) lived at the Anchor Inn on the right-hand side of the road going to Emberton and just on the Olney side of the river.

The embankment in the Park is part of the track for a railway that was to have run from Newport Pagnell to Olney, but the company went bankrupt before it was completed. On June 5th, 1888, a tramway was begun to run from Olney to Newport Pagnell. However, it was never completed, but some of the old tramlines are said to be still in place below the present road surface. An old print in the book "Olney Past and Present" shows them along High Street South.

Clifton Reynes has a long history. In Domesday Book it is spelt in two ways, Clistone and Clystone, the name of Reynes coming from the family who owned the manor. The name Clifton comes from the fact that the village is on a hill. Domesday Book also records that the woods at Clifton could support four hundred hogs.

The church, one of the most interesting in the district, is built in Early English style and is dedicated to the Blessed Virgin Mary. The church was founded by the Borard family before ecclesiastical records began, and is said to have been built in the reign of King Edward I. In the church are two wooden effigies, with no inscription. They are thought to be in memory of someone in the Reynes family, possibly Ralph de Reynes, whose second wife was Amabel, the daughter of Sir Richard Chamberlain of Petsoe Manor. There are ancient tombs to the families of Beaucham, Zouche and Reynes, also one of Sir John Reynes who died in 1428. The Reverend Samuel Pepys was rector of Clifton Reynes, and he died in the same year as his namesake, Samuel Pepys, the diarist. It is thought that they were cousins. There is a slab to his memory in the church. The church was damaged during the Civil War by Cromwell's troops who used it as a stable.

In the village stood the dovecote which has now been destroyed. It was a circular structure built of stone and had a thatch roof and this building was sixty-three feet in diameter.

The school was built in 1844 by the Reverend T. Evetts.

To the north of the church can be seen the site of Clifton Hall, also called the Manor House. This was built of stone about 1750 by Alexander Small. There was another manor called Wake's Manor but where this was situated is not known.

> *"I sing of a journey to Clifton*
> *we would have perform'd if we could"*

Cowper wrote this when he could not get to Clifton Reynes because of the floods.

From Clifton the green lane leads across the meadows to Lavendon Mill. This, too, was recorded in Domesday Book, in 1086; there is another record of the mill dated 1246. The river is now crossed by the new weir and not by the ford which was a few yards downstream.

Of Lavendon Mill itself there is very little left. Corn was ground there until the 1930's. Situated under the hill, the mill house looks across the river and facing south catches the sun, at the same time being protected from the cold northerly winds.

Lavendon Mill was a favourite spot of the Reverend John Newton. He would take tea with the miller, Mr. Perry, and then preach a sermon in the barn nearby. It was in the field close to Lavendon Mill that the poplars stood. When they were cut down Cowper wrote the following:—

> *The poplars are felled; farewell to the shade,*
> *And the whispering sound of the cool colonnade!*
> *The winds play no longer and sing in the leaves,*
> *Nor Ouse on his bosom their image receives.*
>
> THE POPLAR FIELD.

In 1534 there was a quarrel between the Throckmortons of Weston

Underwood and a man called Thomas Hill who had been given permission to wash 400 sheep in the Mill dam at Lavendon Mill. What the quarrel was about and how it started nobody knows.

On July 3rd, 1925, Sir Alan Cobham was taking part in the King's Cup Air Race when he became lost in the fog. He landed in a field at Lavendon Mill where he stayed the night and flew on next day.

From the mill the green lane can be followed to Lavendon Grange, built in 1626 by Robert Eccleston, using some of the material from the old manor, which was an extensive building. Dr. Richard Newton, founder of Hertford College, Oxford, was born near Yardley Chase in 1676. He lived at the Grange for several years. He died in 1753 and is buried in Lavendon church. It is said that Sir Isaac Newton, the great scientist, used to visit the Grange. The Sundial is dated 1626 and has the inscription PEREUNT ET IMPUTANTUR (The hours perish and are laid to our charge).

To the east of the Grange are the remains of Lavendon Abbey, founded in the time of Henry II by John de Bidun in honour of St. John the Baptist. Other accounts suggest it was dedicated to the Blessed Virgin Mary. The Monks were Norbertine or Premonstratensian, also called the "White Canons" because their habits were all white. These habits were said to have been prescribed by the Virgin Mary. The monks were called Norbertines after St. Norbert and came to England about 1140 A.D. settling in Newhouse in Lincolnshire.

St Norbert gathered many disciples. "Seeing the salvation of so many committed to his care he humbly prayed for Divine Direction." It is said that the Blessed Virgin Mary appeared in a vision and pointed out a lonely barren spot in the vale of Courcy in France, called Pratum Monstratum (The Indicated Meadow) and the name was adopted by the community. At that time thirty – five abbeys of the order existed in this country. The abbey at The Grange was just neglected and fell into disuse and was in ruins at the time of the dissolution of the monasteries by King Henry VIII.

The monks were forbidden to eat meat, hence the fish ponds.

An old view of Weston House.

Later they obtained permission from the Pope to eat meat when on
a journey, and later obtained permission to eat it all the year
round except from Septuagesima to Easter. Many skeletons have
been found and legend has it that a duchess lies buried here –
thought to be Lady Basset of Drayton, sister of the Duke of
Brittany. In her will she left instructions for her body to be buried
in the chancel of the abbey. She died in 1403. The last abbot of
Lavendon Abbey was William Calys.

In 1863 a gold epaulet was dug up by a man called Edward
Panter. This was valued at the time at £10 but it was claimed by
the church as it was found on church land. Nearby is a field
called "Fair Field". Lavendon Abbey fairs were held on the festival of the Assumption of the Virgin Mary. Roman and Early
English coins have been found as well as brass Nuremburg card
counters. These were probably used by the monks in games of
skill.

The Hyde, the Courts and Olney Park have practically no
records of their past. The Courts may originate back to Boret,

Another view of Weston House, from an engraving.

30

The "Knobs" at Weston Underwood. *Photograph by the author*.

the Saxon. Olney Park, a parish in its own right, is owned by the
Duchy of Lancaster. In 1374, Ralph, Lord Basset of Drayton,
who was Lord of Olney emparked about three hundred acres,
now known as Olney Park.

In a line south west of the Hyde is the Courts Farm and con-
tinuing in a straight line the village of Weston Underwood is
reached. The name means Western Farm in the wood. There is
a village of the same name just north west of Derby. The village
of Weston Underwood has a close connection with Cowper. Built
on the hill overlooking the valley, it does have some very fine
views. The Park was laid out by "Capability" Brown, and the
village still retains much of the old world atmosphere in spite of
the many alterations of recent years. One loss was the demolition
of Weston House in 1827. Of the house itself little remains. The
Clock House was originally the stables, coach horses at one end
and hunters at the other end, and the enclosed yard was called
locally the 'Jail Yard'. The house at the east end was once part of
the chapel. The pillars at the entrance to the drive of Weston

31

The Alcove after restoration in 1976. *Photograph by the author.*

House still remain as does part of the moat. This was the home of the Throckmortons.

Just past the site of Weston House one enters the village through the pillars of the old gateway. This used to be a walled village and the stone pillars with their ornamentation on top are known locally as the "Knobs". The wall and gate at the other end of the village have completely disappeared. Beyond the old school and the Manor House are the crossroads; the road junction is where the village cross once stood, but all that remains is the base. Turning left down the lane there is a fine stone-built house, for many years the home of the Pater family. Going up the lane the Alcove is reached. This was built in 1753 by Mr. John Higgins for Sir Robert Throckmorton in the shape of a hexagon and from it a fine view of the Park is seen. Gone is the fine avenue of lime trees, as well as the Chestnut Avenue. These were cut down after the first World War, in spite of many protests. Hugh Miller's description of the avenue of lime trees is as follows:

"We have got into a noble avenue of limes – tall as York Minster, and very considerably longer, for the vista diminishes till the lofty arch seems reduced to a mere doorway; the smooth glossy trunks form stately columns, and the branches, interlacing high overhead, a magnificent roof."

His description of the avenue of chestnut trees was as follows:

"There is a long line of squat broad-stemmed chestnuts on either hand, that fling their interlacing arms athwart the pathway, and bury it, save where here and there the sun breaks in through a gap, in deep shade; but the roof overhead, unlike that of the ancient avenue already described, is not the roof of a lofty nave in the light Florid style, but of a low-browed thickly-ribbed Saxon crypt, flanked by ponderous columns, of dwarfish stature but gigantic strength."

In the valley below the alcove the stream which Cowper called the "Weedy Brook" runs down under what was called the "Rustic Bridge", now, for some reason, often called "Devil's Bridge".

The avenue of lime trees.

The stream continues down the valley to join the Overbrook, or as it has been called Over's Brook or again Ho-brook. The stream then runs alongside what is known as the First Spinnie, but called the Shrubbery by Cowper. It was in this Spinnie that the Moss-house stood, being a low stone-built structure with a thatched roof and covered with ivy, and a favourite haunt of the poet.

In the Park and attached to the gardens of the Manor is an enclosure known as the Wilderness, a secluded spot overgrown with trees and shrubs. In it stood the Temple, as well as two monumental urns and other monuments – some put up after the Poet had left the district.

Back in the village the public house "The Cowper's Oak" is passed and just beyond stands a fine stone house called "Stone-ways". Beyond this is another called the Lodge; it was here the Unwins lived and where Cowper stayed from November 1786

The Moss House in the shrubbery.

Weston Lodge from an old engraving.

Cowper's Oak, September 1882. *Photograph by R. G. Scriven.*

to July 1795. It was on one of the window shutters of his bed-
room in this house that Cowper wrote the words:

"Farewell, dear scenes, for ever closed to me;
Oh, for what sorrows must I now exchange ye!"

This was written just before he was due to go to East Dereham in
Norfolk, on July 22nd, 1795. The original shutter from his bed-
room is now in the museum still with the original writing on it.

Just outside the area described in this book is the tree known as
Cowper's Oak. This is reached by the concrete road through
Yardley Chase at Olney Lane End. In this area are many fine old
oak trees. Unfortunately, the tree known as Cowper's Oak, or
Yardley Oak, was destroyed by fire some years ago. There were
two more very old trees called Gog and Magog. The tree called
Gog used to be called "Judith", a name by which it had been
known from time immemorial. The tree is said to have been
planted by the Lady Judith, a niece of William the Conqueror and
the wife of Earl Waltheof. There was at one time some confusion

about which was Cowper's Oak, and which tree was called Judith, the confusion arising from a letter from Dr. Johnson of Norfolk to Mr. Hayley. This letter has confused Hayley and many other people since, but from Cowper's own description it is quite clear.

The trees called Gog and Magog are larger than Cowper's Oak. Gog measured thirty-two feet in girth and five feet from the ground. Magog measured twenty-nine feet in girth. Cowper's Oak measured twenty-two feet six-and-a-half inches. In about 1880 Gog was fifty-eight feet tall and contained 1550 cubic feet of timber, while Magog was sixty-nine feet tall and contained about 1500 feet of timber. Both these trees are figured in "*Silva Britannica*" published by J. G. Strutt in 1822.

Cowper in one of his happier moments wrote a poem about the Yardley Oak, in 1791, but it was never finished and he never published it. It was Hayley who found the manuscript and published it. The poem contains the lines:

> *"A giant bulk,*
> *Of girth enormous, with moss-cushioned root*
> *Upheaved above the soil, and sides emboss'd*
> *With prominent wens globose"*.

Nearby is Kilwick Wood and Dinglederry (the name Dinglederry is given to a new housing estate in Olney; it is also the name of a pond in the field opposite Clifton Pastures) originally belonging to John Throckmorton and is part of Yardley Chase which itself was part of the great hunting forest stretching from Whittlebury Forest and probably joining up with Rockingham Forest. Cowper's poem the "Needless Alarm" has the lines:

> *"With the high-raised horn's melodious clang*
> *All Kilwick and all Dinglederry rang"*.

Weston Underwood now has a village green, once the site of a row of thatched cottages which stood with the backs to the road and called the "Burrough". Farther along the road is a large house which stands at an angle giving it a view along the road. This used to be called "Pear Tree House" and at one time was the Curatage, where the Reverend Thomas Scott lived. He paid his rent in the form of a basket of pears to his landlord, Charles Higgins, and was duly given a receipt. When Hugh Miller visited Weston about 1872 he remarked on the number of grape vines growing on the houses, also that due to the bad summer the grapes were no bigger than currants.

Just beyond is the church said to have been built by John de Olney in the 14th century. Once the church was attached to Olney church as a chapel of ease. In 1376, after many requests, a bull (an edict by the Pope) was issued permitting it to be a church in its own right, as it was more than a mile from Olney and when the Overbrook was in flood it was difficult to attend services in Olney, or for a funeral to get through the floods. Later a wooden bridge was built. The church is built in the Perpendicular Style and is dedicated to St. Lawrence.

At the back of the church are some stone coffins or covers to coffins. Leaving Weston and returning to Olney a good view of the river valley is seen.

> *"Ouse, slow winding through a level plain*
> *Of spacious meads with cattle sprinkled o'er,*
> *Conducts the eye along its sinuous course delighted."*

Descending the hill past the Spinnie can be seen the view well known to Cowper – this view is shown on a plate in the Cowper Museum. The landmark here is the fine beech tree on top of the hill. From here one can see across the river to Emberton and looking down the river can be seen the river bridges and the extreme south of Olney, while looking upstream the river can be seen going towards Filgrave. Along here is a wide stretch of river known as the "Broads" and beyond this is the "Island" on which is the heronry.

> *"The Ouse, dividing the well-watered land,*
> *Now glitters in the sun, and now retires,*
> *As bashful, yet impatient to be seen."*

COWPER.

The most spectacular view was when the river was in full flood, providing a wide stretch of water as far as one could see. These meadows used to be wet and marshy; to overcome this Dutch engineers were brought in to drain the water off. This was a problem as the meadows are below the level of the river. It was accomplished by draining the water from the meadows through a pipe under the river to discharge the water into the pool below the weir. With the new weir flooding will not be seen only in exceptional circumstances, nor will be seen the frozen flood waters with hundreds of skaters, the braziers with hot chestnuts, and the entrepreneurs who took a chair on which one could sit and have one's skates fitted for one old penny. Any quantity of snow brought out the toboggans when the young and the not so young could enjoy themselves on the hillside.

CHAPTER FOUR
A later history of Olney

Carrying on from where we were at the end of the last chapter, leaving the beech tree and going towards Olney one gets a good view, albeit a spoilt one, of the south end of the town. Where there used to be green fields there are now council houses. All this against a backcloth of Clifton Hill to remind us how much we depend on nature even with our present-day technology. As one descends the hill there can be seen on the right the old stone bridge over the river. This is called "Goosey Bridge" and is now a rather unsafe structure for heavy vehicles. The other bridge is called Toone's bridge leading into Toone's meadow, this meadow being surrounded by water. The pool near the bridge is a favourite spot for swimmers in the warm weather, and a good spot for fishing, although somewhat of a hazard in a boat trying to get under the bridge when the river is in flood.

Nearby, enclosed in a wire fence, is a marshy area known as the "Sway Gog" so called no doubt owing to the fact that it vibrates underfoot when walked upon. Always a place to be avoided it has a reputation tied up with Olney Devil-lore. It is said that one night the Devil drove into Olney from the Warrington Road. His chariot was drawn by four headless horses, and driven by headless coachmen. It drove into the "Whirly Pits" and emerged out of the "Sway Gog" having reached it by an underground passage. There are other versions about coaches and headless horses using the underground tunnel. In fact, there are many stories about the Devil who seems to have visited the town many times and is said to have stayed on occasions. The story goes that he used to visit the Two Brewers public house frequently. It is said he used to stay at a big house on the site of 121 High Street. Here he was annoyed by an old lady who put her head out of her window to watch him, but one day when she was looking at him he caused a large pair of horns to suddenly grow out of her head so she could not withdraw through the window. When she promised not to look again he made the horns disappear.

As we pass the "Sway Gog" there is on the right-hand side of the road the entrance to what is known as the Tan Cutting, a pathway leading to Lime Street. Just at this point there is a depression caused by the extraction of clay to make bricks. This is still called the Brickyard. The bricks here were hand-made and the small cottages which used to be along the Cutting were called the Brickyard Cottages. Opposite are the council houses on what used to be the allotments, behind which was a field called the Feoffee Field. This field had a small pond in it where one could always catch a newt, a great pleasure for small boys. At one time a muddy stream ran down the Weston Road probably fed by the springs breaking out on Weston Hill. It went down the road past the lamp-post and then turned south to join the river. It is not sure whether it followed the road or went to the rear of the houses in High Street South.

Coming down the Weston Road, which used to be called Dagnel Lane or Dagnel Street, there are the Alms Houses and the British School. These buildings were erected in 1819 and endowed by Ann Hopkins Smith who was a member of the Society of Friends, more often known as the Quakers. She lies buried in the old Quaker churchyard near the remains of the Quaker chapel at the back of the Gas Board offices in Silver End. The British School, now a factory, was used for many years as a meeting hall as well as being used for concerts and social gatherings. The author's grandmother used to talk of "spelling bees" being held there. Various teams would compete under a Chairman, – in those days it was a popular form of entertainment. She told the story of one member of a team who, when asked to spell cuckoo, spelt it out in his usual deliberate manner, c-u-c-k-o-o, after which he was saddled with the nickname of "cuckoo." He had the last laugh, he was the best speller!

A short way down the road is Lime Street, which used to be

British School, Olney.

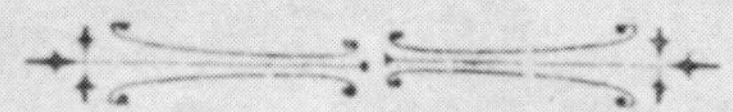

A LECTURE

Entitled :—

" My Experience of New Guinea and its
Savage People,"

Illustrated by a large number of **Beautiful
Slides**, shown by a powerful Lantern,
will be given by

James E. Liddiard, Esq., F.R.G.S,

On Thursday, October 11th, 1906.

———

Chair to be taken at 8 p.m. by the
REV. S. H. SMITH, M.A.

———

A Collection will be made in aid of the
Funds of the Society.

Notice of a lecture in the British School advertised in the "Free
Churchman."

Gargoyle on the building in Lime Street. *Photograph by the author, by kind permission of Mr. R. F. Soul.*

called "Dead Lane", because funerals from Weston Underwood used to pass down there on their way to the Church. The late Mr. Charles Hipwell had the lime trees planted and the name changed to Lime Street.

In the building now used as a garage in Lime Street can be seen two gargoyles which, no doubt, came from the church during the alterations in 1807. Also, it is thought that, at one time, a nunnery stood somewhere here, as pieces of dressed stone are found in some of the old walls round about.

Going on down the Weston Road there is, on the right, the old thatched building which used to be the Sun Inn and opposite and over the stone wall used to be Dagnall House. During the second world war Sir Aylmer Firebrace used to visit his friend Colonel Coke who lived in Dagnall House. Sir Aylmer will always be remembered as the man who organised the Auxiliary Fire Service ready for air raids. Where the road joins the High Street stands the "Alleluia" lamp-post, so called because of the singers who used to sing underneath the light. There were the Salvation Army, whose meetings round the lamp-post gave it its name, the Carol Singers at Christmas Time, also the Male Voice Choir, not forgetting the Town Crier who usually stopped there to call out

44

Weston Road from an old print in the author's possession. *Photographed by the author.*

his notices. His bell is now in the Museum and is brought out for the starting of the Pancake Race.

Turning right the road narrows and on the left is the Swan Inn, an old coaching house. Across the road is an architectural gem in the old bakehouse, the date on the front being 1717. The bow-fronted window is a good example of Georgian design. The wooden doorway to the house was taken from Weston House when it was demolished. It is pleasing to note that as these words are being written a start has been made on restoring and preserving this property.

Just beyond the Swan Inn is the house where Thomas Wright used to live, and the big room at the back is where he had his school. This was called the Cowper School for Boys. Day scholars under twelve years old paid twenty-one shillings for a quarter, while boarders paid six pounds for a quarter. Well known for his books and great interest in Cowper, he could be seen on a Monday morning going round the town to collect his rents. In appearance he dressed and looked like Charles Darwin. Mrs. Wright was the principal of the Cowper School for Girls.

Then comes the Church Hall. Once the National School it was divided into two sections, the boys on the left side and the

Bridge Street, Olney, in 1976. *Photograph by the author.*

girls on the right. In front, along the pavement, stood a low wall with iron railings, the area between the school and the railings being the playground. The playgrounds were entered under two stone arches partly of local stone and partly of Northampton Sandstone. These arches were closed by gates. Now the building is used as a meeting hall, the centre division having been taken away, as well as the railings and arches. Opposite is what is now called "Tory" Row. This was originally the Workhouse Yard, the inmates being dressed in white flannel swallow-tailed coats, leather breeches and dogs' skin caps.

Following the main road along Bridge Street, originally called Brigge Street, the Salvation Army at one time had a Citadel in a hall at the back of the house known as "Sunny Side" (previously it was the Golden Lion public house), and alongside the path leading to the Church. The Salvation Army was quite active, its strong supporters being people named Aldridge and Linger. The Hall, besides being used for a short time by the Catholics, was

The Church Hall, from an old photograph.

The Friends' Meeting House.

Tomb of the Rev. John Newton; the memorial to his father-in-law is on the left. Note the gargoyle in the wall behind the tomb. *Photograph by the author*.

The Great House, from an old illustration.

later used by the St. John Ambulance Brigade, and the Boy Scouts.

At the end of the houses in Bridge Street, there is an entrance to the Churchyard. From here one gets an appreciation of the Church tower and spire which together are 185 feet high. The weather cock is about two feet nine inches from beak to the tip of the tail and about two feet high. On it are the words: "I never crow, but stand to show, whence winds do blow, 1829." The curved sides of the spire give it a fuller effect, straight sides to a spire giving it a hollow backed appearance. This curvature is called 'Entasis' – a word originating from the Greek language. Entasis was found in some of the columns of the Ancient Greek Temples.

The Church has a peal of eight bells, the oldest dated 1532.

"Tall spire, from which the sound of cheerful bells
Just undulates upon the listening ear."

COWPER. TASK I.

On the South side of the churchyard is the grave of the Reverend John Newton who, with Cowper, wrote the Olney Hymns and nearby is a memorial stone to his wife's father, George Edcott. Newton's gravestone is a massive block of polished Aberdeen granite weighing ten tons. Going on and through the gate, Church Street is reached, leading down to the site of Olney Mill burnt down on November 16th, 1964, and previously destroyed by fire on January 3rd, 1878. Between the church gate and the mill once stood the "Great House", thought to have been in existence in 1624 and the mansion in which King Edward IV was taken prisoner. After many years of habitation it was used as a workhouse and gradually fell into decay. Mathew Marriott was the last keeper of the old workhouse. Of the house itself little remains but the two pillars at the entrance to the north gate of the churchyard; these were presented to the churchwardens and removed from their original position to where they are now. A fireplace was also removed and put into the Mill House.

At the east end of the church where the brick cottages stand the

High Street South, Olney, showing the tram lines. From an old print.

day school was opened on June 25th, 1819.

Coming back up Church Street the Vicarage is reached, looking very much as it did when John Newton lived there. It was the Rectory until 1504 and has been the Vicarage ever since. It was during his stay there that it had extensive renovation.

On October 11th, 1852, the Vicarage was nearly destroyed by fire when an oil lamp fell and set the stairs alight.

Near the church is the field called Lordship Close and it was here, near the churchyard wall, that the Parish Cross stood, the base of which remained until about 1880. It was at the foot of the village cross that deals were sealed with a handshake, especially for people who could not write.

Olney was known for its courts. These are often narrow passages or roadways, sometimes a cul-de-sac, at others a thoroughfare. In these courts were usually several cottages. Leaving Church Street and going along the main road the first of these courts is reached, opposite the Alleluia lamp-post at the rear of 20 High Street South. This was called Osborn's Court. At one time about

The Bull Hotel, The building in the shade beyond the hotel was the Saracen's Head. *Photograph by the author.*

fifty or sixty people lived in the cottages here. In one of the cottages lived "Dicky" Fennell and his wife, who had no children. In the other cottages were large families such as the Harris's and the Tarry's; how they packed them into the tiny cottages is a mystery. As well as courts there are "yards", such as "Clicker's Yard", "Hawley's Yard"; there is also "The Leys" at the end of West Street.

Across the road from "Alleluia Lamp-post" is the site of the house where Mr. Teedon lived, where the optician's premises are at the moment. Teedon's diary has been published by Thomas Wright and the original diary is in the Cowper Museum.

Approaching the Market Square, on the left is the Bull Hotel, an old coaching inn. The servants of the travellers who put up at The Bull had to use the public house next door, the Saracen's Head. The Market Square is of a triangular shape, so turning right and going along the south side Cowper's House, or as it was called "Orchard Side" is reached. This house was given to the Town of Olney and the Nation by Mr. W. H. Collingridge on

Cowper museum. *Photograph by the author.*

April 25th, 1900. It was given with the hope that it would be used as a library and museum of Cowper's work. This has been done and the museum is now thought to be the best on one person and his work, in Europe. At one time Orchard Side was tiled, but it is said they were removed and replaced by slates while the tiles were sold to an American.

When Cowper lived there he used to walk from the garden at the back of his house across an orchard to get to the vicarage to visit John Newton. In order that Cowper could do this, rather than walk along the street, Newton paid one guinea a year to allow Cowper to cross the orchard and ever since this has been called "Guinea" Orchard. A visitor to the museum can see the pew taken from the church, which Cowper used, also the summer-house can be visited. Here in this peaceful spot Cowper could sit and write, or take his visitors. One of these visitors was the Reverend William Bull of Newport Pagnell who came about once

Cowper's Summer House in 1976. *Photograph by the author.*

a fortnight. In the summerhouse can be seen the loose board in the floor, under which it is said the Reverend Bull kept his pipe and tobacco.

"While clouds of income half divine
Involve thy disappearing shrine;
And so may smoke-inhaling Bull
Be always filling, never full."

COWPER.

A previous owner, a Mr. Aspray, who was an apothecary, is said to have kept some of his bottles in this cavity. The interior of the summer house is now covered with signatures of visitors. One name on the west wall is that of Hugh Miller, the geologist, who wrote "First Impressions of England", "Testimony of the Rocks" and "The Old Red Sandstone". Another name is that of John Tawell of Great Birkenstead, Hants., who was hanged for the murder of his mistress on the 21st July, 1842.

In the book "First Impressions of England" can be found a detailed description of Weston Underwood and Olney. It seems that Hugh Miller put up for the night at the Duke of York public house, now a newsagent's opposite the Working Men's Club. The original date stone can be seen on the front of the house. As he had been walking all day he asked the landlord if he had anything to quench his thirst. He had taken a drink at each runnel (stream) and wanted something not so heady as ale, on which the landlord produced half a dozen jargonelle pears. The landlord remembered Cowper and had a slight recollection of Thomas Scott. During conversation with him Miller found he (the landlord) was the last of the race of Old English yeomen found in this part of the country. Miller's book was published in 1874 and it is interesting to note that Miller caught the omnibus to Wolverton. It was horse-drawn, of course. An advertisement dated 1869 states an omnibus started at the Bull Inn, Olney, at 7.30 and 1.40 only except for Sundays.

In the garden at the back of his house Cowper had a greenhouse. It was in here that he wrote "John Gilpin" and much of "The

The elm tree in the centre of the market square. *Photograph loaned by Mr. C. R. Mann.*

Task". This greenhouse has since disappeared. Cowper wrote that it had been converted to a summer parlour and it was in here – especially in the summer – that he spent a good deal of his time. He wrote "The sound of the wind in the trees and the singing of the birds are much more agreeable to our ears than the incessant barking of dogs and screaming of children." In the past, references to the greenhouse have been confused with the summerhouse.

The market square now has a different look about it than in the past. There used to be three big elm trees, one right in the centre with iron railings round it. This was the last tree to survive. It is said the trees were planted to celebrate the three kingdoms of the United Kingdom unified in the reign of James I. Under the centre tree were the stocks. Not so far away was the Shiel Hall, the upper storey of which was a meeting room, and also called Teedon's School. An entry in Teedon's diary for July 1st, 1793, says that a Mrs. Orsborn came to ask about her son going to school. An entry on July 8th, 1793, states Charles Orsborn came to school. Another entry date January 4th, 1794, is that Mrs. Osborn came and paid for Charles – in this entry the R is dropped.

The Shiel Hall (Teedon's School) and the Round House, from an old engraving.

Olney market, 1976. *Photograph by the author.*

The word 'Shiel' is unusual as it is a Scottish term. This room was reached by stone steps on the outside of the building and part of the ground floor was used as a smithy. The building was demolished in 1816. Also on the square stood a small octagonal building. This was the "Lock Up", sometimes called the "Round House" or the "Stone House" and was demolished in 1846. There were other buildings on the square. It is said that cottages actually stood on the square in Cowper's time. Also, there stood on the square what might have been called the Parish pump, a cast iron construction which had a gas lamp on top and drew water from a shallow well close by. The pump stood about where the entrance to the market square car park is now. The pump is now in the garden of the Museum.

On the Market Square is the War Memorial inscribed with the names of the fallen of the two world wars. This was built in 1921 and unveiled by General Horne.

Near the Bull Hotel on the west side of the square – at present an antique shop – is where the printing premises of Oliver Ratcliff were and it was here that his books on Olney were printed, such as "The History and Antiquities of the Newport Hundreds" and "Olney with its wit and humour". Much of the type for the book on the Newport Hundreds was set by Alfred Page who, in his later years, worked for the author. Before he died Alfred Page gave to the author his personal copy of the book, inside which is a coloured plate with the words: "Presented to Alfred Page by his Master, Oliver Ratcliffe. Christmas 1901". The "Olney Advertiser" was printed here; locally known as the "Buster" it was first published in 1897.

Just along the road is the Sutcliff Baptist Church. In 1814 it was named after the Reverend John Sutcliff who was a minister in Olney for thirty-nine years. The history of the church is an interesting one, though very little is known of its early days. The date 1669 seems to be found in all Baptist handbooks. It is thought it could be because in that year Archbishop Sheldon requested all clergy in the Canterbury province to provide him with evidence of "Unlawful religious assemblies". Against three such assemblies the name of John Gibbs appears. These were held at Newport Pagnell, Newton Blossomville and Olney. The assembly at Olney was held at the house of Widow Teare, which was in what is now Weston Road. About two hundred people were there, and it is said they were "meane" people. They were led by "John Gibbs, and one Breedon and James Rogers, lace buyers, and one Fenne, a hatter".

If the persecution of the Dissenters was severe, meetings were often held in the area of Threeshire Wood at Warrington. It was easy to escape the forces of law by crossing the boundary to another county. It was here also that dog-fights, cock-fights and prize-fights took place.

John Gibbs had the distinction of being the first minister ejected from his living. He was ejected in 1660 two years before the great ejectment of those ministers who refused to conform. Various reasons are given for his dismissal. One is because he refused communion to the Squire when the Squire was drunk; another more favoured explanation is that he upset Sir George Booth,

The Baptist Chapel before being restored.

later Lord Delamere. At the restoration Sir George Booth had his revenge being "a man of very bitter spirit".

There is no doubt that John Bunyan preached in Olney, probably on the Market Square and also in Joseph Kent's barn which stood on the site of the present chapel. The chapel was built in 1694 and enlarged in 1763 and completely altered in the 1890's. Some of the lower courses of the old building can still be seen. There used to be a door leading to the garden next door and to the house now known as Westlands where John Sutcliff lived before he moved to 20 High Street. The Reverend Sutcliff was one of a

59

High Street, Olney, 1976. The first house on the right was one in which the Rev. John Sutcliff lived. *Photograph by the author*.

committee of five who founded the Baptist Missionary Society. Tradition has it that the society was founded at the house in the High Street, although officially the beginning of the mission was at Kettering, with Sutcliff as the main personality. The man who actually started the missions was William Carey who had studied at Sutcliff's academy. In fact, twelve of the early missionaries studied under Sutcliff in Olney before setting out to do their work in places like India, Ceylon and the East Indies. Dr. William Carey was a member of the chapel from July 14th, 1785, to April 29th, 1787. He was born at Pury End, Paulerspury, and died in 1834.

The Reverend John Sutcliff was buried in the graveyard of the chapel. His grave is one of the few that are left, the rest have had their gravestones removed in order to make a lawn. There is an oak tree grown from an acorn from Cowper's Oak which was planted by William Wilson on January 1st, 1800. William Wilson was Cowper's barber and he, too, is buried in the Baptist graveyard.

Near the Chapel the corner shop used to be a clock and watch-makers; opened in 1809 by George Hollingshead it was carried on through four generations.

It was in 1712 that the Congregationalists finally broke away from the Baptists. The Cowper Memorial Chapel (now the United Reformed Church) was built in 1880 on the site of an earlier structure built in 1700 and approached by an archway from the High Street. Where the church and the Working Men's Club now are, used to be a row of cottages extending from Millard's Entry to the Two Brewers' Public house. It was due to a large extent to the efforts of the Reverend G. G. Horton that it was possible to build the present church. The church was badly damaged by fire in 1965.

The High Street retains much of its character; the stream is no longer there, nor is the causeway which used to run from the Swan Inn to the top of Midland Road. The causeway was necess-ary because of the terrible state of the roads. It was maintained with money from the Causeway Charity. The Causeway Charity and Pierson's Charity combined to form the Feoffee Charity. It is not known how, or where, the Causeway Charity originated. Pierson's Charity originated from the will of Richard Pierson, who, in his will dated July 12th, 1626, left £150 to the poor of Olney. A deed dated July 4th, 1649, states "In the seventeenth year of the reign of Charles, late King of England, the Court of Chancery ordered the purchase of land". On May 14th, 1677, more land was purchased for £29 and paid for by the people of Olney, for the relief of the poor of the parish.

In the nineteenth century there existed the Ladies Clothing Society which helped the poor by the distribution of clothes.

The main road is part of the old turnpike road from Newport Pagnell to Cold Brayfield and Bedford, and the High Street is said to be one of the five widest High Streets in Britain. The late Mr. William Garrard was the last person who had the sole right to shoot duck on the stream running down the High Street.

In 1777 and 1854 there were devastating fires in Olney. The latter fire burnt fifty houses and damaged thirty more, all at the

Sunday School Anniversary,

SUNDAY, JULY 22nd, 1906.

Preacher:

Rev. P. H. Smith,

College St., Northampton.

Services, 10-30 a.m. and 6 p.m.
United Service in the Afternoon at 2.30.

Collection for Sunday School Fund.

The School Treat will take place the following day at Ravenstone, by kind permission of Mr. George Nicholls.

Tea for Friends at 6d. Each.

Advertisement of the Sunday School Anniversary in the "Free Churchman", 1906.

north end of the town. Most of the houses were thatched, but this has now been replaced by slates and tiles. Recent work on some of the roofs has revealed scorchings on the stone wall and, in one instance, some of the charred thatch in between the stones. Other fires occurred on August 8th, 1831; January 4th and April 8th, 1853; March 23rd and June 26th, 1854, and one in 1786 which destroyed forty-three houses.

The fire on January 4th, 1853, was caused by incendiaries who were at work in the town. This was a serious fire resulting in the deaths of three men. William Scott and John Marson were killed by the collapse of the building when they were trying to rescue belongings from the burning building, while Jacob Clifton was terribly burned and died later as a result of his burns. The person, or persons, responsible for the fires at this time were never found.

To raise money for the relief of the dependants a series of ballads by local people were printed and sold.

One of the "Fire Ballads" is printed here. It is the work of Henry Collingridge.

VOICE FROM THE ASHES OF THE LATE FIRES AT OLNEY, BY AN OLNEY BOY.

When danger seems to threaten least,
*   And we appear secure from harm;*
How oft the sad and sudden change
*   To sorrow and alarm !*

The year was drawing to a close,
*   That happy season too was near,*
When friends with friends in love do meet,
*   To share their joy, to sooth their fear.*

How many a face was bright that eve,
*   With love, and joy, and hope;*
How many a heart did warmly beat
*   With danger unprepared to cope.*

But hark ! one single cry transforms the scene,
    As sadly ringing through the air;
A word prepares the joyous mind,
    For the frightful, furious glare.

In jealous spite, or fiendish rage,
    Some rude and ruthless hand;
Had set on fire a stack of corn,
    With match or fiery brand.

Not long had this event passed by,
    Than one occurred more fearful still,
Some buildings then were set on fire
    The work of that same wicked will.

Four January days had run their race,
    And darkness veiled the sky;
When again we heard that fearful shout,
    "Fire ! fire ! and danger nigh".

The alarm had scarcely yet been given,
    Before the flames their lengths had cast
On corn, and cattle, wood and straw,
    And in their grasp did hold them fast.

Beyond the rest two men were seen,
    To strive, to help, to save;
Whate'er was good and moveable
    From fierce and fiery wave.

Not heeding much their danger,
    On, on, they worked intent,
Till with a crash the roof gave way,
    And then two souls their lives had spent.

Not further will I trace this scene,
    It has been done so well before;
By the voice of Muskett, and Dix,
    Of Brittain and of many more.

But let me add my modest mite,
  To value charity and zeal;
And earnest praise with feeble voice,
  The heart that can for others feel.

"Weep for the brave," we'll say again,
  While thinking of the dreadful fate
Of Marson, Clifton, and of Scott,
  For whom all caution is too late.

Think much of their virtues, their failings forget,
  And do what we can to help all distress:
The look for reward in a mind free from care,
  And one that would ne'er condescend to oppress.

In another fire seven cattle were burnt to death. This was on December 31st, 1852.

A large second world war-time fire was at the tannery on the night of Monday, February 28th, 1944. This was thought to have been caused by a ventilating fan. At this time the black-out was in operation, and it was a very dark, cold night. A vivid memory was the sight of the church floodlit in red by the flames, and standing out against a black sky.

There was a remarkable coincidence about this fire. At that time many firemen from the north of England had been drafted down to the south of the country in preparation for "D" Day. At Wolverton were stationed many crews and appliances from Manchester. In order to keep them occupied and in training, exercises were held in the district. A full scale exercise was held at the tannery on Sunday, February 20th, 1944. It was decided to assume some of the buildings had caught alight and could be prevented from spreading by defending fire obstructions, like the end wall of a building. The whole exercise was carried out as the real thing, pumps were set in at the river and water was pumped on to the buildings. Eight days later those buildings were on fire – each crew knew its job and what to do!

The large building in the High Street with the words: "Bucks. Lace Industry" on it was built by George Knight in 1928 on the orders of Harry Armstrong, who was a lace dealer. Mr. Armstrong came from Stoke Goldington. At the Empire and Imperial Exhibition in 1911 he was awarded the gold medal for his display of lace. The building was built with second-hand materials. This meant the design was governed by the size and amount of material available. The site on which it stands used to be that of the house of "Johnny Pater", who was a coal, coke, cake and salt merchant as well as an Agricultural Contractor hiring out steam ploughing tackle and thrashing machines. His telephone number was Olney 10. The house was completely burnt down on the night of February 11th, 1923.

Carrying on towards the north end of the town, the Knoll is reached with the Castle Inn, one of the oldest inns in the town, obviously getting its name from the nearby site of the castle. Looking at the front of the inn there used to be on the right side a smithy, where, until the 1930's, horses were shod and the ring of

Olney Railway Station.

the anvil could be heard over much of the town when the wind was in the right direction. The Knoll was often used as a meeting place for people living in the area, especially for political meetings. This and the Market Square, were the places for these meetings before electioneering became so sophisticated.

"The noisy man is always in the right".

COWPER

Dartmouth Road was named after Lord Dartmouth who owned a large part of this district and was a benefactor on many occasions. This area of the town may be the oldest part and it does follow the pattern of many Northamptonshire villages. Also, it was here the first church stood, an early Saxon church probably not much better than a barn. Wellingborough Road, Midland Road and Newton Street are modern, many houses bearing the date of their construction. The old Queen Hotel at the top of Midland Road was built for the travellers on the railway. One could leave horse and cart there to be looked after by the ostler and then walk down the road to the station. Newton Street used to be a short cut across the fields to the station. The corrugated iron buildings, now the Ambulance Hall, used to be the Wesleyan Chapel, and under the Patronage of the Wesleyan Bromham Road Chapel in Bedford. The houses in East Street, which make up what is known as Warwick Terrace, were built by apprentices working under supervision.

Warwick Terrace in East Street and Beauchamp Terrace on the Knoll undoubtedly take their name from the Beauchamp family who were the Earls of Warwick. In 1403 the Manor of Olney came into the possession of Richard Beauchamp, Earl of Warwick. The ancestors of the family came to England with William the Conqueror. It is interesting to note that in Down House, the home of Charles Darwin, can be seen the genealogical table of the Darwin family. These ancestors include the Beauchamp family, the Earls of Warwick, though admittedly a very tenuous connection.

Beyond Wellingborough Road, and just beyond where the railway arch was, is the road junction to Lavendon. It was on this corner that the gallows stood. Also, about here, is buried a man called Marryot who committed suicide at the Saracen's Head next to the Bull Hotel in 1790. The story goes that if you walk round the grave at midnight and can say the Lord's Prayer backwards without a mistake an apparition of Marryot will appear. Along the Lavendon road is the site of Dropshort or Dropshot and it was here that the pest house stood. Much of East Street is old, and some of the old stone walls and houses can be seen today as well as some of the tiny brick cottages. At the south end of East Street is the site of the old Olney Gas Works, where gas was produced for the town. The town was first lit by gas on September 21st, 1854, and celebrated by a dinner at the Bull Hotel on September 27th, 1854. In the wall surrounding the gas premises can be seen a small wooden door, too small for an adult to crawl through. This was put there so that the Fire Brigade could put their suction pipes through into the well on the other side of the wall. At one time there were two doors, one farther along the wall towards East Street. This last one has been filled up, but one can see where it was in the wall.

Along East Street can be seen "Fairfield Close" which is the site of the old fair field. Olney fairs were granted in 1315 and could be held on Easter Monday and on June 29th, the festival of St. Peter. The fair held in June is called the Cherry Fair. There is also a fair listed for October 13th.

From the gas works it is a short distance to the Market Square, and the area between is called "Silver End". In the book "Olney and the Lace Makers" published in 1864 it states: "One of the outlets of the Market Square is Silver End, the St. Giles of Olney." St. Giles is the Patron Saint of Cripples and lived in the sixth century A.D. St Giles day is celebrated on September 1st. In Cowper's day it was rather a rowdy area, and the children there caused him some annoyance. Although not actually in Silver End, Cowper, described his house as being "deep in the abyss of Silver End". Just beyond Silver End is the Old People's Home called "Clifton Court". Before this was built there was a row of brick cottages called Timpson's Row. In one of the cottages lived a farm worker called Jack Huckle, one of the good old school of countrymen, who had a beef pudding every day. At that time six-pennyworth of beef and one-pennyworth of suet made a good meal.

West Street has been altered much during the past few years. It is now the area of two new housing estates, also Spring Lane has been widened and extended to the council houses on the Weston Road. It is only in the past few years that it has been possible for traffic to go up Spring Lane and come out in the Weston Road. The avenue of chestnut trees that stood at the back entrance to Westlands has now disappeared, no longer do the schoolboys collect their conkers here as they used to.

The large brick building in West Street is the Convent, building for which started on 19th March, 1903. In 1381 John de Olney purchased land at Weston Underwood and from the Olney family it passed by marriage to the Throckmorton family in 1446. The Throckmortons were Catholics and, after the Reformation, services were held in a room used as a chapel in Weston House. When this was demolished Mass was said in the Granary until a chapel was built. In 1898 the estate passed to Major (later Colonel) Bowyer. The last Catholic service in Weston was held on 20th March, 1899.

After this, services were held in Olney at the old Liberal Club. This was where the Old Folks' Club now is in the High Street. Then services were held in a hall in Bridge Street, previously used by the Salvation Army. Eventually two acres of ground were purchased in West Street where, in 1900, a temporary church was built. The Priest's house was built in 1901.

It was in 1902 that laws imposed by the French Government caused some religious orders to leave the country. In October of that year three nuns came to Olney and rented two cottages opposite the present Catholic Church. They were soon joined by six more nuns and eventually established a Convent. All these young Sisters had already received an excellent education in France and all they had to do was to translate their knowledge into English and win academic teaching diplomas from various teachers' training colleges and also degrees from Oxford University. All the Sisters did this with remarkable success.

Later their numbers were increased by qualified British Sisters.

Then a Roman Catholic elementary school was opened. At the same time a High School was started which carried on until recent years, although the elementary school was closed after the First World War. Another service rendered by the Nuns to the district was a dispensary where people could get free medicine. A Sister with the necessary qualifications came to the Convent on May 2nd, 1904, for the purpose of visiting the sick, either in their own homes or in the dispensary attached to the Convent. An article in "The Olney Advertiser" read as follows:—"One of the Sisters of Saint Joseph's Convent, who has had many years experience in nursing has opened with the approval of the local doctor a small room in one of the outbuildings of the Convent where she will be ready to attend, free of charge, to any case which might be brought to her and which does not require the doctor's attendance, or which may be sent by him." The author has recollections of going to school there as a small boy and being given some cough mixture. Whatever it was, it tasted nice!

Exploring the town one finds the "Courts" already mentioned, the names of the others being "Swain's", "Cobb's", "Flood's", "Morgan's", "Field's", and "Berrell's". The spelling of the last is shown by the name over the court today. Normally, the name, an old Olney name, is spelt Berrill. Cobb's Court is named Cobb's Gardens. This may be because of the gardens to the cottages. There are houses on one side only, the gardens are on the other side of the court.

From the Market Square to "High Arch", that is to the arch leading to Cobb's gardens, was the whipping distance for offenders. Their hands were tied to the back of a cart and as they walked behind the cart they were whipped all the way there and all the way back.

Besides the names mentioned above there are many names of Olney families that can still be traced back a long time, three hundred years or more.

CHAPTER FIVE
More Modern History

The explorer will also find some large buildings, one of which is at the south end of East Street, having a peculiar square projection to the roof at one end of the building. This is where the kiln was. These are the old malt houses which belonged to the brewery; there used to be five of them and the largest was at the back of the Two Brewers' public house and was used during the last war to dry grain that had been damaged by water in the dock fires and the grain was then used for animal food. One of the others still exists at the back of the Old Rose and Crown and can be seen at the bottom of Berrells Court; another, in the High Street, is now used as a lampshade factory. There was one more at the back of the Old Boot Inn in Bridge Street but this one was not used a great deal.

At the back of the Bull Hotel is a large building, now a furniture factory. Originally this was the brewery run by the Hipwell family, started by William Hipwell who came from The Swan at Newport Pagnell. This closed in 1916. The brewery chimney was taken down as it began to lean and was thought to be unsafe. The chimney was built with bricks made at the brickworks at the Hyde. Many of these bricks were dated about 1880, the date being imprinted on them in manufacture, but no trace of these can be found. Underneath the building are large cellars which were used as an air raid shelter during the last war, also some of the cellars and the buildings above were occupied as stores for fire brigade equipment. They were stored here rather than in London because of the 'Blitz'. Another part was used as a cattle grading centre during the rationing period.

The large brick factory at the top of Midland Road was originally a single-storey shoe factory, the second and third storeys

The malting at the back of the old Cock Inn. *Photograph by the author.*

being added later. During the last war it was used as a factory to make sparking plugs for aeroplanes; now it is used as a book warehouse. The brickwork of this building and that of two old cottages in Spring Lane is said to be some of the best in the town.

Olney, like many other towns and villages built on, or close to, the Jurassic limestone that outcrops in a line across England from Dorset to Yorkshire, uses this material as a building stone. Almost all of the old buildings are built of it, as well as many walls that divide various premises. In some places the stone does show signs of weathering, but in other buildings it is still in very good condition and as good as the famous Helmdon Stone.

Many houses do have a smooth stone facing; this is a dressed Oolitic limestone that was obtained from the quarry at Warrington. Some of the cut stone used for facing was probably imported into the town. The recent renovation to the church was carried out with Weldon Stone, a nice oolitic freestone from a village near Corby in Northamptonshire. Many years ago there used to be the quotation:—"Olney on the Oolite", the phrase probably originating from Hugh Miller's book "First Impressions of England".

Unlike many towns Olney does not display the exotic stone often found on bank, insurance, building society offices, and town halls. This is a good thing. These foreign rocks, while producing a fine appearance to a building, are really not in keeping with a small market town. The Church does have some Caen stone in the reredos and the font is made of it; there is also some "Devonshire Marble" – this is actually a limestone.

There are no exotic doorsteps in the town, but most of them are made of what comes under the heading of "York" stone. This is a Permo-Triassic sandstone quarried in the North Midlands. This stone is also used to cap the wall on the front of the Almshouses. Many local doorsteps are made of concrete but only a very few are made of local stone.

In the town itself most of the thatched roofs have gone since the great fires, slate and tiles replacing the thatch. In many of the older brick buildings much use has been made of the different coloured brick; the stretchers or bricks laid longways being the red colour, the headers are bricks laid crossways, a dark purple. Laying bricks in this manner is termed "Flemish Bonding". This made an attractive pattern. One of the few imported stones is found on the Church Hall and surrounding wall; this is the Northampton Sandstone and possibly came from Duston. Considering how near the source of this stone is, it is surprising that not more was used. Some more is found on Orchard House in the High Street. There are a few pieces incorporated in the wall round the churchyard. The corbels on the end wall of the farm house known as Town Farm at the end of the High Street near the Knoll are made of this stone, and two large pieces are on each side of the gate to the house on the corner of the road leading to Clifton Court. It is also used a little in the construction of Emberton, Clifton and Weston Underwood churches. Some is used in the walls in Weston Underwood. Going up Cross Lane one large piece is used in the stone wall round the Wilderness. The wall between Guinea Orchard and the Vicarage has coping stones of this material. One of these big flat stones had a hole cut out in it with a piece of sandstone to fit the hole like a cork in a bottle. There was a small cavity underneath, but what it was used for nobody seems to know.

Many of the old gravestones are made of this stone, but the weathering has all but obliterated the inscriptions. The oldest stone in Olney churchyard is said to be inscribed Robert Sharp and dated 1667.

Missing now are the cobbled pavements. At one time many of the yards and courts were surfaced with hard brown quartzite pebbles. These pebbles were laid with the aid of a "Pitching hammer". This was a long piece of wood with a handle on the side and the bottom was ringed with a piece of iron to stop it splitting. One hand was placed on the side handle, the other hand held the top of the piece of wood and this was used as a rammer to knock the pebbles in firm and level. The pebbles were replaced by blue bricks, and now the bricks are being replaced with asphalt. A small area of cobbles can be seen in the front of what used to be the Saracen's Head public house near to the Bull Hotel.

Around Olney will be noticed about four houses with an oval cast iron plate on them. On the plate is the inscription "O.F.P. 1845". The letters stand for Olney Feoffee Property. The houses are owned or were owned by the Feoffee charity at some time.

Much of the character of the High Street is due to the houses, most of them being of a different height or type of construction from their neighbour and no two roofs are pitched at the same angle. Some of the older houses have a steep pitched roof but these were probably thatched roofs at some time. An additional attraction is the decoration on the eaves of many of the houses and much work has gone into this. There is none of the ribbon building of the Victorian Era, nor at the moment any of the modern steel and concrete structures.

Over a long period of time Olney has never been what might be called a prosperous town. Indeed, in days gone by, it was said to have been a poor and depressed place, by all accounts. In 1832 cholera broke out in Silver End. Twenty-two people died and most of them were buried by the Reverend H. Gauntlett. In the time of the Reverend John Newton smallpox broke out in the town.

At the same time, with the distinctive character of the town the inhabitants, too, had their own typical character and their names and deeds are still recited in the homes and public places.

The shoe industry did not become the main industry until after the great fire of 1854. The first factories built in Olney were built by a Mr. S. R. Owen and a Mr. G. A. Drage. Hinde and Mann started their business in 1890, afterwards building the factory at the top of Midland Road. The factory of S. Cowley Ltd. which was a single storey factory at the back of the houses at the bottom of Yardley Road was burnt down one Sunday morning in 1926. The other shoe factory was that of Mr. T. Johnson in West Street and at the time of writing is still being used. Much of the shoe work was done in the homes of the workers. The older inhabitants tell how the shoe workers used to get drunk; when the money had run out they would start work again and repeat the process all over again. Later, machinery took over much of the work previously done by hand. The first sewing machine in Olney was sent to a shoemaker, Thomas Harris, whose premises were later burnt down. The first rivetted shoe made in Olney was made in the workshop at the back of 94 High Street, by S. R. Owen. As well as making shoes, leather was made at the tannery as it still is. Leather made in Olney is some of the best produced in the country. It is interesting to note that William Carey was a shoemaker at Moulton before studying under Sutcliff and later becoming a missionary.

Today there are fewer shops, few public houses, and the town is not so self-sufficient as it was, even at the beginning of this century. The following list of Trades is from Oliver Ratcliffe's book printed in 1907.

Boot and Shoe Repairer	Hairdresser
Bird Specialist	Plumber
Baker and Confectioner	Tailor
General Stores	'New Hall' for entertainment
Wine and Spirit Merchant	Gas Company
Monumental Mason	Expert Pigeon Breeders
Draper	Engineering and Cycle Works

Convent School

Shoe Manufacturers

Builder

Furniture and Cycle Dealers

Bespoke Shoe Makers

Milliner

Butcher

Grocer

Builders' Merchants

Watchmaker

Fancy Draper

Wheelwright

Millers

Fishmonger

Dressmaker

Confectioner

Saddler

French Polisher

Carpenter and Undertaker

General Stores

Window Cleaner

Antique Dealer

Music Teacher

Steam Plough and Threshing Machine

Tanners

Printer, Bookbinder, Stationer and Numismatist

Building Contractors

Basket Makers

Ironmongers and Bucks. Pillow Lace Accessories Dealers

Dairywoman

Coachbuilder

Billposter

Corn Merchant

Chef

Coffee Roaster

Coal and Wood Dealer

Sweet Shop

Dairyman and Fruiterer

Toys and Tobacconist

House Decorator

Besides these there were the professional people, such as the doctor, lawyer, clergyman and dentist.

Many of the above had sidelines such as picture frame makers, haberdashers, caterers, coke, granite and slag merchants. One notable exception is that of the chimney sweep! There must have been some then.

The chemist is not mentioned. In 1869 the medical and dispensing establishment was owned by a Mr. W. Fever where "Physicians prescriptions were carefully prepared and duly copied for reference".

Looking at the list there is no mention of the lace industry, other than Sowmans who advertised accessories for lace making. The story of lace making is written by Thomas Wright in the book "The Romance of the Lace Pillow". Some of the early lace makers arrived in Kent in 1563 having fled from Philip II of Spain who, at that time, ruled the Low Countries. Another influx of lace makers was in 1685 when Louis XIV revoked the Edict of Nantes. Many of these people settled in this area, especially in Bedfordshire – particularly in Cranfield. One interesting note is that the first wooden bobbins were made at Sharnbrook in 1616, the continental lace makers using bone bobbins. The making of wooden bobbins is said to be England's contribution to lace making. Many glass beads on the bobbins were made at Cranfield. They are square and were hand-made, showing the marks of the flat files between which the beads were formed.

Millward's Entry is so called because a man called John Millward lived in the house where the entry is, at the side of the United Reformed Church. This man designed lace and made the parchments for the making of lace. Bucks. Point Lace used by Queen Victoria at her accession was designed by John Millward and made in Olney. William Soul, a friend of John Millward, was also a lace designer. Millward had a club foot and Soul walked with a stiff arm action. Locally they were disrespectfully called "Pendulum Bill" and "Dab foot". Olney has always been noted for its nicknames.

The glassworks used to be at the back of 14 High Street. In the possession of the grandfather of the late Mr. 'Ted' Hollingshead was a glass ornament made at these works but it seems to have disappeared. Number 14 at one time belonged to a stone mason, the garden at the rear being the stone-mason's yard. The business was run by James and Edward Andrews, who also had the glass blowing business. These brothers were also responsible for many of the quaint carved head-stones in the churchyard.

Another important trade in Olney was that of the baker. In 1812 the only bakers were Thos. Dumviles, Jo Todd, John Soule and Thos. Davidson. Toward the end of the century there were ten bakers: Parrott in Bridge Street near where George Knight now lives; Brooks at the bakehouse in High Street South; Waters who had one oven in the Weston Road where the Little Shop (opposite Lime Street) is and another in East Street near where

John Millward receiving the congratulations of Olney friends on winning the golden award at the Great Exhibition of 1851. Standing (left to right): John Millward, Lace Manufacturer; William Soul, Lace Designer; Rev. James Simmons, Baptist Minister. Sitting: Wm. Killingworth, Watchmaker; Thos. Aspray, Doctor (London). *Photograph loaned by Mr. C. R. Mann.*

Fairfield Close is now; James Aspray in the corner of the Market Square, this being sold to another baker S. Hill; Rabans on the Square where Turners' Ironmongers shop is now and who were bakers for about one hundred years; Soule next to Orchard House who had a long record (workhouse records show purchases from them to the beginning of the 19th century); Whitmee at the top of Midland Road; Thomas Osborn (the great-grandfather of

the author) at 20 High Street South who died on April 4th, 1883 –
although hidden behind an office wall the arches of the ovens are
still there, in fact, that room was called the bakehouse up to the
time the business was closed in 1972; Swains where Swains Court
is; and John Walders at 35 High Street where the Estate Agents
now is. Besides these there was a baker in Emberton who delivered in Olney and so did two bakers from Lavendon and one
from Weston Underwood – they all seemed to make a living!

In the days of horses and carts an important trade was that of
the harness maker and saddler. There used to be two in the town –
Arthur Harris at 77 High Street who had a branch at Stoke
Goldington and also attended at Hanslope; the other saddler was
Mr. Walter Ratcliff whose shop was where the Olney Antique
Porcelain Company now is and the branch establishments were
at Yardley Hastings and Turvey. When Mr. Ratcliff retired, his
business was taken over by John Harris, son of Arthur Harris.
It was important in those days that harness was kept in good order,
especially heavy harness for working horses.

The business of basket makers was carried on by the Smith
family for something like two hundred years. There used to be
Sidney Smith and his father, then Dan Smith, and "Joby" Smith
and two brothers Robinson. These worked at the actual basket
making, or tending the Osier beds, planting, cutting, and producing the osiers for the business. There used to be a hut standing
along the Wellingborough Road on the left just beyond the old
railway arch, and it was in this hut that women and children were
employed peeling the osiers. At one time the basket making used
to be carried on at 94 High Street, before moving to 22 Bridge
Street. The story goes that one of the members of the Smith
family at that time was fond of home brewed beer and did, during
a dry period, dam the brook in the High Street in order to collect
water for his brewing!

In the course of time some of these trades have died out or have
been concentrated into large combines, but at the same time new
industries have come in. Through all this time agriculture has
played a great part; through good times and bad the farms in the

area have produced food for the people. Whatever happens to other industries it seems this industry will carry on.

In the list of trades carried out in Olney will be seen the 'New Hall'. This was built for the purpose of entertainment by Mr. Lewis Thompson who had a grocer's shop next to Barclay's Bank. Later the hall was converted to a cinema, first for the silent films, then the "Talkies". What a thrill that was! Then after that the colour films arrived. The cinema was run for many years by Mr. and Mrs. Alistair Bull. Mr. Bull was the last blacksmith in the smithy next to the Castle Inn. The cinema has now been converted to a shoe factory.

The cattle market was re-started before the first World War by Messrs. Foll and Bawden, in the position where it is still held today. Bawden was the auctioneer and Foll did the clerical work. Between the two wars the consignments of livestock ceased. Besides the cattle market a poultry market was held every Thursday, when poultry, eggs, butter, rabbits and quite often furniture was sold. "Moss" Hedge was the auctioneer. A Christmas Show was held when pens of Rhode Island Reds, or Light Sussex or some other favourite breed of poultry were exhibited. Prizes were also awarded for Geese and Ducks, as well as for butter and eggs.

The Christmas Fat Stock Show has continued throughout and has drawn support from a wide area.

There was a cattle market in the time of King Edward II. In 1307 it was an important market. At that time the Crown had the right of pre-emption, that is, it could buy up provisions at its own valuation regardless of other purchasers. In June 1317 Robert Legat and John Salcote were convicted of obtaining sixty head of cattle by forging a commission with a counterfeit Royal Seal. They obtained these cattle from the market town of OLNEYE. They were tried and Salcote was sentenced to be hanged but Legat was acquitted.

In those days cattle were driven long distances by drovers who would rest the cattle overnight and move on again next day. In order to stop the night there were fields where the cattle could be enclosed. These fields were often long narrow strips of land. There

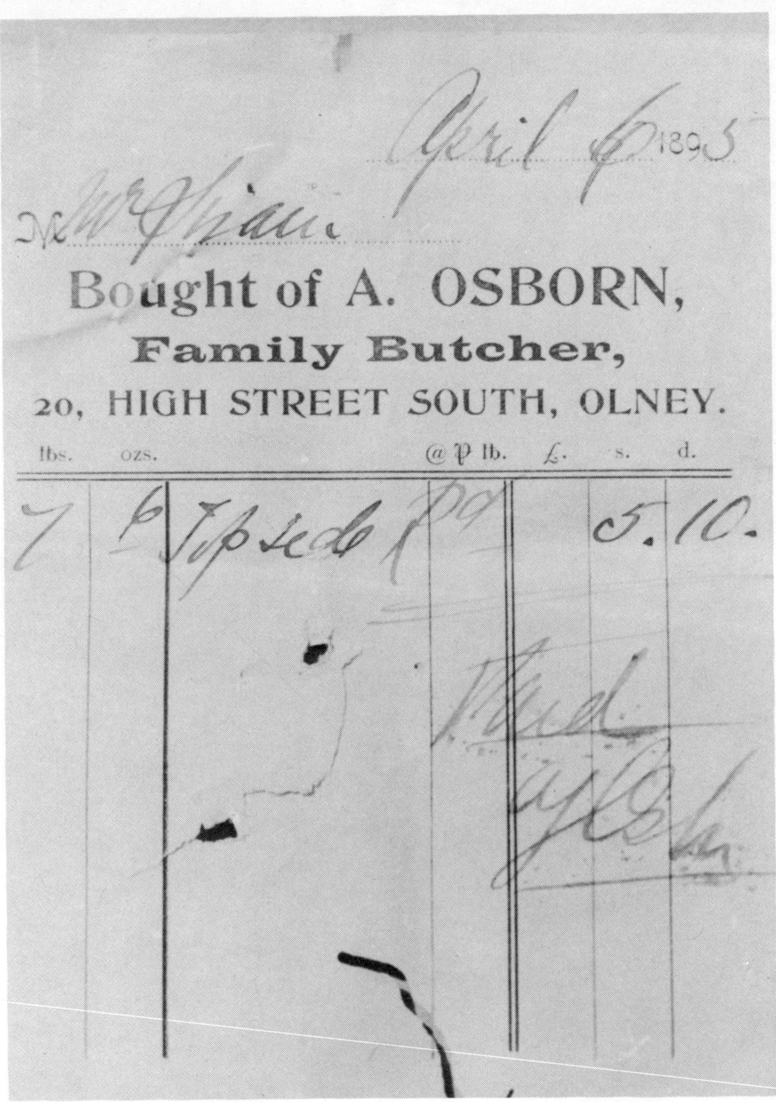

The "Good Old Days": topside of beef 9½d. per lb. (about 4 new pence).

is one on the road to Yardley Hastings, opposite the entrance to the Court's Farm, and another is along the road from Ravenstone to Ravenstone Mill. Some cattle were driven from Wales to the market at St. Neots now in Cambridgeshire. Cattle were also driven from Scotland to Smithfield or Smoothfield as it was called. These cattle, often the Galloway breed introduced by the Vikings, were sold in London. A yearling steer would fetch eight pence, a two year beast would make one shilling and a penny, while a milking cow would make two shillings and two pence.

CHAPTER SIX
Organisations and Local Customs

As with many other towns Olney has its local organisations. Among the sports clubs the Olney Rugby Football Club was established in 1876. Other sports such as Football, Tennis, Bowls and Cricket have been played for many years. There are also the Women's Organizations, such as the Women's Institute and the Mothers' Union as well as various groups attached to the other religious denominations. The Friendly Societies have a tradition of long service. The Boy Scouts and the Girl Guides have done good service among the younger generation. The Scouts were started in 1906 by George Knight with "Johnny" Minard as the first Scoutmaster. "Johnny" was one of those tough people who went swimming in the river all the year round. The Scouts were called the 16th Bedford troop. A Mr. Evatt, editor of the "Beds. Times", was the District Scout Master. Since the First World War there has been the British Legion – the Men's Branch and the Women's Section. This has now been given the prefix of Royal. The Pre-school Playgroup was formed in 1968 and the Floral Fiesta was introduced in 1965.

This story cannot be told without mentioning the Fire Brigade and the St. John Ambulance Corps.

The Fire Brigade was founded on October 19th, 1878. Mr. M. A. Booth was the first Captain and Mr. W. M. Hoskins was the Secretary. In the early days it was a horse-drawn team. The horses had to be taken out of whatever vehicles they were drawing, taken to the fire station and hitched on to the fire engine, or worse still, if the horses were out to grass somebody had to go and catch them. Later the fire engine consisted of a manual pump towed by a charabanc owned by the Minney Brothers in the High Street, after which a Daimler car once owned by the Farrars' of Chicheley

Olney Fire Brigade about 1921; the two horses belonged to Pratt's Petroleum Company (the name was later changed to Esso). Petrol was delivered by horse and cart in two-gallon cans!

Hall was converted and did service for many years. It had no foot accelerator, the head-lamps were acetylene and the side lights were big brass candle lamps. Before the Second World War a new Ford chassis was bought and the old body transferred to this.

The Brigade carried out many war-time tasks, and saw service at Coventry, Bristol and Portsmouth, as well as supplying crews for relief and back up duties during the air raids. Another duty was to supply a relief crew to the forces waiting for "D" Day. Since the War the Brigade has moved to new premises in East Street. Before the war, and during the whole of hostilities, the Brigade was housed in the old premises at the back of the Two Brewers' public house. In the days of the old converted Daimler the Brigade used to drive up the yard at the back of the Two Brewers and under the archway into the High Street. The arch still exists on the front of the public house. The building on the south side of the arch, now part of the public house, was once the Mechanics' Institute, later the Olney Club.

The Ambulance Corps was founded in 1896 and since that time has given wonderful service to the area. A founder member was Mr. W. T. Knight who had a shoe shop at 14 High Street. He was Secretary and First Officer. Dr. F. J. Grindon was Olney Divisional Surgeon, and President of the Committee was Mr. Arthur Hipwell who lived in Gresham House. A Mr. Leapidge Cooper had much to do with the Ambulance in the early days. At that time patients for the hospital were put on a wheeled stretcher and wheeled to the railway station. When the train stopped at Northampton they were then wheeled to the hospital. The first motor ambulance was a model "T" Ford. Later a new ambulance was purchased, the money being raised with the help of public subscriptions and this was used until the National Health Service took over.

One sad loss is that of the Olney Town Silver Band, disbanded before the war. Its instruments were ignominiously carried away in the dust cart. Olney has a tradition of music. There was Dr. Henry John Gauntlett who was born at Wellington in 1805 and was six years old when he came to Olney. He was the son of the Rev. Henry Gauntlett. Dr. Gauntlett was a distinguished church musician and has been called the "Father of Church Music". In more recent years music in Olney has been kept alive especially by the Kitchener family. Older readers will remember the male voice choir singing carols at Christmas time. Some will also remember the Olney Choral Society, founded 22nd September 1903, by Mr. W. W. Wright who was church organist and after he gave up the baton it was conducted by Mr. Britton of Emberton. The Society had nearly sixty members.

For many years the first Sunday in May was called "Hospital Sunday" or "Band Sunday". On that Sunday afternoon a procession headed by the band would march from the top of Midland Road to the church for a combined service. The collection taken in church and in the street was in aid of the hospital funds. For the parade every organisation turned out; behind the band were the members of the parish council and other local dignitaries, followed by the various organisations – even the cubs and brownies took part. For the spectators it was time to show off their new spring fashions; all in all, it used to be a great day.

The town has long been noted for the Pancake Race said to have been first run in 1445 but the origin of the race is obscure. Revived in 1924 as a joke by a few ladies living near the church and always run on "Shrove" Tuesday it is now run in competition with the town of Liberal in the United States and now many other towns and villages have taken up the idea. On August 21st, 1871, the Olney and Emberton boat race was held, but whereabouts on the river and who won is not known.

A custom that has died out is that of "Plough Monday". On the third Monday after Christmas the agricultural workers and some who were not agricultural workers, would dress up in their smocks, black their faces with burnt cork and go round the town knocking at the doors and chanting:—

> *Poor old ploughboy*
> *Gi'us one ha'penny*
> *Only one, only one.*

This they would keep up until a response would bring the reward of one halfpenny.

Another dangerous custom was carried out on Guy Fawkes night, the fifth of November. A tow ball was made, consisting of a bundle of rags. This was soaked in paraffin, then lit and kicked round the town. It caused more than one fire. One was kicked through the window of Bass's the drapers in 1872. This was where Barclay's Bank now is.

Olney has been represented for many years by a Parish Council, and recently has been granted the status of a town with the chairman of the council having the title of Mayor. Early this century the council was divided into two factions – one known as the "Ba-Ba gang" whose members were mainly liberals and non-conformists, and the "Black Hand Gang" the members of which were mostly directors of the Olney Gas Company.

In 1869 there were the following societies and clubs in Olney:—
The Wellington Club, patron the Right Hon. the Earl of Dartmouth. The President was the Reverend J. P. Langley, Vicar of Olney. Then there was the Olney Amicable Society which met at the Boot Inn. The Chairman was Mr. Charles Talbot. There was also the Oddfellows who met at the Two Brewers' Inn. There was the Victoria Benefit Society, the Church of England Book Society and the Cowper and Newton Book Society. There was also the Working Men's Institute. "Public Schools" are listed as the National School and the British School.

Artistically Olney has been associated with Charles Spencelayh, the artist and painter, who moved to Olney during the first World War. He was born at Rochester and studied art in London and Paris. His first wife was a girl who went to school in Olney with the author's grandmother.

During the first World War he was living in London when during an air raid by the zeppelins, a German airman was shot or fell out of the aircraft and crashed through Charles Spencelayh's conservatory. This upset him so much he moved to Olney. He resided at No. 8 High Street where he set up his studio in the building at the back of the house. Back in London during the Second World War he was bombed out in 1940 and this time moved to Bozeat.

He had the distinction of hanging more pictures in the Royal Academy than Sir Alfred Munnings; in fact he hung pictures there for over fifty years.

One of his earliest pictures was the famous painting which advertised Colman's mustard.

As a painter of miniatures he was a master. A portrait of King George V, the size of a postage stamp, was painted by him and hung in Queen Mary's dolls house. One of his treasured possessions was a letter of appreciation from Queen Mary written in her own hand, about the painting.

Modern transport now means the district is not so isolated as in years gone by. On the other hand, it is easier for people to get here. It is hoped these visitors who come either for business or pleasure will leave the town with pleasant memories and a renewed interest in the British Countryside.

The new city of Milton Keynes now being built will have some influence over Olney and the surrounding area. Having survived for hundreds of years it is hoped this threat, too, can be warded off and a way of life preserved that is the envy of urban dwellers.

CHAPTER SEVEN
Natural History

The area so far described, although small, has an abundance of wild life both animal and plant.

Birds of all sorts are abundant. There is a heronry at Filgrave, already mentioned, while during the winter many waders make use of the wet meadows. Years ago when the meadows were in flood for much of the winter many birds, especially migrants, would take advantage of the flood and the marshes to make a stop, sometimes for a short stay, at other times staying for weeks.

With the lakes at Emberton Park and a much more enlightened attitude towards wild life, more water birds than ever are here. The lakes now have a permanent population of duck, grebe, coot, and moor-hen, and the occasional visit from the swans. Similarly, the river has its own population. Careful observers can see the kingfisher. Many snipe can be seen, especially during the winter, and the redshanks arrive in the spring to nest. In the early spring many people keep a sharp look-out for the swallows to arrive, one of the earliest dates for them here being March 31st.

Animal life, too, has its share. Rabbits and hares are common although the rabbit population does vary with the spread of myxamatosis. Stoats, weasels, watervoles, and hedge-hogs are common as well as the smaller mammals, such as the field mice, shrews, voles and moles. The dormouse is very scarce if it exists in the area at all. The harvest mouse can still be found. The otter is occasionally seen in the neighbourhood but it is now very scarce. Neither the edible dormouse nor the yellow-necked mouse are found here at present, although they do occur in the middle of the county.

Foxes are common and badgers are found. While rats and mice are always present especially around farm buildings. The last black rat seen here seems to be the one killed in the Tan yard on March 7th, 1870. On the higher ground towards Yardley Chase fallow deer are often seen as well as the muntjac.

The beautifully marked and harmless grass snake is more common than for the past few years. The common lizard can be found. but the slow worm does not seem to be found any more. No adders have been reported here. In common with much of the country frogs are now scarce. At one time thousands of frogs could be seen in the meadows in the early summer, but toads are now more numerous.

The river, ever popular with the fishermen, contains many good specimens of freshwater fish such as bream, roach and pike. Salmon are no longer caught although there are records of them being caught in the Middle Ages. The occasional tench is landed, and crayfish still inhabit some parts of the river. It was said at one time that carp could be caught in the Whirly-Pits. In 1933 the All-England Fishing Contest took place in local waters.

There is a good selection of plant life, the old railway cutting and the verges of the roads having a varied flora. The meadows and springs provide a damp habitat for those plants that need moisture. The spring opposite the Green Hill on the Weston Road supported a prolific growth of stonewort, that is, before it ceased to run during the drought. The higher ground provides a rich lime soil, evidence of this being shown by the "Old Man's Beard" or wild clematis growing in the hedges, while in other places the clays provide a habitat for plants that do not need so much lime. The old stone walls often have a covering of moss as well as the pretty toadflax with its tiny flower, while in the early spring the yellow stonecrop gives a splash of colour on many walls and roofs. Lichens do not grow well in this area due to the atmospheric pollution. A few common species are found on some tiled roofs or on stone or concrete.

The elms have suffered greatly, few are left, and some of these may soon be infected with the Dutch Elm Disease. There are still many other trees common to the English countryside as well as a few exotic species that have been introduced. There is a mulberry tree at Emberton and one in Olney. Also at Emberton is a fine Cedar of Lebanon with the flat top peculiar to the species, as well as an Evergreen Oak and an Atlas Cedar. In Olney can be found the Giant Redwood trees imported from America, about 1873. In those days it was the thing to do to have one or two of these trees growing on the estate. In the churchyards can be found the yew trees, once so necessary for the making of the long bow.

Insect life is less numerous than it used to be, the dragon flies and the damsel flies are much more scarce. The large brown aeshna can be seen occasionally hawking up and down a hedgerow or over the water as it searches for its prey. One does not see any more the "Blue Mist" over the river caused by millions of damsel flies flying over the water on a fine day in early summer, nor are the mayflies as numerous as they were.

Many species of butterflies have vanished, although the recent fine summers have helped them and there have been some success-ful second broods. The peacock butterflies are more numerous as are the brimstones. The common blue which used to be seen in thousands in the Weston Road meadows is now only seen in a few scattered colonies. The Camberwell Beauty has recently been seen, while the Purple Emperor may still be about.

Other insect life is varied, the river and the lakes providing a habitat for the aquatic larvae of many insects, such as the caddis flies. The moths are numerous; a light on a fine summer's night will soon attract many species. The delicate "Golden Eye" can often be found in the house, and a walk round the garden on a fine summer's day will provide a display of many beautiful and useful insects. The old stone walls provide a home for the miner bees, who in the early spring can be seen looking for a suit-able spot to burrow in the soft cement to make a nest. The grass-hoppers once very numerous can still be found occasionally.

As well as the useful and beautiful insects there are the more noxious types. The horse flies can be a nuisance in the meadows during the summer, drawing blood if they can get their "beak" into your flesh. Mosquitoes have suffered from the dry weather, their breeding places have dried up, making life much more pleasant. Yardley Chase was the tenth British locality to yield that viscious biting mosquitoe *Aedes vexans*. Fleas are much more common than most people realise. Here six new species have been added to the county list. One new specimen has recently been found in Emberton Park in a coot's nest. This does not mean there are more fleas in this district than in other places, all it means is that somebody has looked for them here!

Other creatures that are not very popular with the general public are the slugs and snails. Out of a list of 199 British non-marine species, 91 species have been found locally. The so-called Roman snail or edible snail is not found here any more. While this snail was possibly eaten by the Romans it was in the country before they arrived. It is much more common in the chalk areas of south-east England. It was last reported at Gayhurst, and used to be found in Northamptonshire.

A search on the hill below the Beech Tree reveals many species of snails, among them the tiny blind snail, the only British relative of the World's largest land snail found in Africa. The beautiful "Banded Snail" is found on the hill as well as at Weston Underwood. The river is thought to be the best in the country for fresh water molluscs, from the large swan mussel to the tiny rams' horn snail. Not quite in the area is the elegant lapidary snail, the nearest known colony of this species being at Horn Wood, Bozeat.

THE SNAIL

To grass, or leaf, or fruit, or wall,
The snail sticks close, nor fears to fall,
As if he grew there, house and all
                Together.

Within that house secure he hides,
When danger imminent betides
Of storm, or other harm besides
                Of weather.

COWPER.

If the weather is suitable the field mushrooms can be picked in many fields in late summer. On the roadsides can be seen the Shaggy Caps and sometimes there can be found the strange but edible morchella.

And as autumn approaches and the leaves change colour, the beauty of the spider's web covered with droplets of dew adds to the natural scene.

One must not forget the microscopic life that teems in the river and ditches. Examination under a microscope shows that these waters contain countless millions of organisms all playing their part in making the living world of today. Some good many years ago an old naturalist said to the author: "Boy, you haven't seen the colour green until you've seen the desmids". The desmids are microscopic fresh water plants, all single-celled and of many shapes and designs, often objects of great beauty. Having seen these many times under the microscope one can only say how right the old man was. Along with the desmids are found the diatoms, possibly some of the most beautiful of microscopic objects. All these and many others are found here by the million.

All this living material from the largest animal to the smallest living organism depends on the weather and the rain in particular. This area does not suffer the extremes of weather that some parts of the country do. It misses the worst of the storms, and lying low as it does – Olney is only about 50 metres above sea level – it is often below the snow line. There can be snow in Yardley Chase, or in Bedford, brought in by the cold east winds, or the Chiltern Hills can be covered with snow when there is none here.

Generally thunderstorms avoid the town, if they come from a south-westerly direction the storms often divide before they get here, part going towards Northampton while the rest follow a path over Emberton and Rectory Farm towards Hardmead. If a thunderstorm does settle in the valley it is usually short and sharp. Olney people say that if a storm comes up over the church it will be a bad one.

During the winter the low lying areas can be troubled by fog and if there is a frost, those gardens on the east side of the town can be damaged, while those on the west side of the town can sometimes escape.

From the hill on the Weston Road there can be seen a wide expanse of sky. From here one sees the mighty cumulus clouds that threaten thunder, or the dark ragged rain clouds discharging their load on the countryside below. Again on a clear dark winter's night the stars can be seen with the Milky Way stretching across the sky, all these with the moon, the meteors and the man-made satellites passing overhead providing a source of wonderment to both young and old.

And so we reach the end of this story of a tiny piece of England, with its history, its hills and hollows, and with its plants and animals, making a world completely divorced from the troubles that beset us today.